Predators:
Reflections on a Theme

Published by
St Edmunds Publishing

Copyright © 2016 John Garbutt

John Garbutt has asserted his right
under the Copyright, Designs and Patents Act 1988
to be identified as the author of this work.

Email
johnw.garbutt@outlook.com

ISBN 978-1-53956-488-1

A CIP catalogue record for this
book is available from the British Library.

Pre-press production
eBook Versions
27 Old Gloucester Street
London WC1N 3AX
www.ebookversions.com

Disclaimer

This work has no connection with any films with titles such as *Predator* (US, 1987), *Predator 2* (US, 1990) and *Predators* (US, 2010); with the novel *Predator* by Patricia Cornwell; or with any video games or military equipment so named.

Predators:
Reflections on a Theme

John Garbutt

St Edmunds Publishing

Introduction

Part I   In the wild

Glimpses of the animal world, where survival is what counts. These are the carnivores, not the herbivores. Judgement on how predators of most species kill for survival is set aside, because the animal world is 'not ours' and is essentially being true to itself. Some oddities lend a few touches of humour.

Part II   In cities and towns

An identification parade of the most serious offenders against the laws of our own species and the laws of our own society. Here are some of the human predators who made front-page news with horrific crimes. Each of these infamous individuals carries the hallmark of 'a deficit of empathy'.

Part III   In human conflict

Man's inhumanity to man: catastrophic events on a large scale, some coming near to the present day. The focusing of power centres: in dictators, in ideologies and in armed forces, each operating with 'a deficit of empathy', though the background differs in each case. Here you meet some prominent rulers including two emperors, a pope, a prince, three dukes, a count, military commanders and some undistinguished people who found power suddenly placed into their own hands. The sequence ends with a review and an Epilogue: a quartet of pieces on remembrance.

Contents

Epilogue

Notes and Acknowledgements

Appendix   205

List of illustrations

Part I

1. Brown bear catching salmon, Alaska
2. Blue dash dragonfly (cf Emperor dragonfly, *anax imperator*)
3. Humboldt squid (*Dosidicus gigas*), in fishing boat
4. Emperor Scorpion (*Pandinus imperator*)
5. Killer whale (*Orcinus orca*) hunting sealion pup
6. Young Barn owl (*Tytos alba*)
7. Sea turtles (*Chelonia mydas*) coming ashore in Hawaii

Acknowledgements

Image No. 19 is reproduced courtesy of Royal Collection Trust, © Queen Elizabeth II (2015); 15, 20, © The Trustees of the British Museum; 9, 10, 11, 12, 13, Getty Images; 17, 18, Bridgeman; 1, 2, 3, 4, , 6, 7, 8, 23, Shutterstock; 5, 21, ImageSource; 16, GraphicStock; remainder, the author.

The author also wishes to acknowledge the kind permission of Arrow Books to quote from Stephen Fry's *The Ode Less Travelled*. Thanks also to the BBC for permission to quote from Alistair Fothergill, reprinted by kind courtesy of *Radio Times*.

In *The Ode Less Travelled*, a volume of wit and wisdom on the essentials of verse by Stephen Fry (Arrow Books, 2005), the first of the Golden Rules to be followed is this:

'As a general rule, poems take time. As with a good painting, they are not there to be greedily taken in at once, they are to be lived with and endlessly revisited...

'We are perhaps too used to the kind of writing that contains a single message... Poetry is an entirely different way of using words and I cannot emphasise strongly enough how much more pleasure is to be derived from a slow luxurious engagement with its language and rhythms.'

Part I:

In the wild

Ye may kill for yourselves, and your mates, and your cubs
   as they need, and ye can;
But kill not for the pleasure of killing, and *seven times never
kill man*!

The Law of the Jungle –
'How Fear Came', from 'The Second
Jungle Book', Rudyard Kipling

Their world, not ours

Hip Hop! My resident blackbird pounces,
Plucks at his helpless worm, and dances.

The barn-owl stares unblinking, rotates his moonface;
Knowledge and night vision inform his genes.
Midnight!   He's off hunting for harmless mice.

Flippety-flappety drum the feet of a thousand gulls;
Each gull commands
A space on the sands
At low tide,
Rehearsing a scene
From a tap-dance routine?
Next day by the harbourside
I crunch underfoot a thousand empty shells.

Observe the peregrine falcon, the master-predator:
Stationary, mid-air, he hovers like a silent helicopter,
Sensors locked on to the mole in the undergrowth,
Intent on each rustle, each quiver of the long grass,;
His prey already possessed in his hyper-insight;
Stored energy summoned, he stoops;
Against this killer-calculator, what chance?

The hawk attacks my dear little blue-tit on the wing.
Black-headed gulls fall from the sky like Stukas
To snatch the elegant avocets.
They gobble up their tasty eggs and chicks.

Challenging the cliffs, the lesser black-backed gulls
Swoop down in raids on their cousins' nests;
And in the Azores, half a million hungry birds
Patrol the richest feeding-grounds
Where the shearwater makes his deadly mackerel-dive
With auto-foldback wings to slice the wave;
Below, the multiple mackerel bait-ball
Writhes in defence and revolves,
Each fish synchronised in the swarming host,
In a single instinct, with one collective mind,
Shifting like singers in close harmony,
Till scattered by the yellow-fin tuna
Darting in feeding-frenzy and co-ordinated attack;
Dispersed and easy pickings for these harrying hunters,
And for the bird-beaks plunging like showers of spears
Ripping and shredding the unprotective element;
While whole communities of dolphin are heading
Away from cold Atlantic regions to the warm Azores,
Bound for their seething, swirling sardine-feast,
Abundant food, perfect prey, one species for another;

While in his privileged pre-eminence,
Haunting and hunting the reefs of the Pacific,
There noses ORCA, the Killer Whale,
Most feared, the mighty marauder
Who knows what's best to eat:
He culls a grey seal for its oily meat,
Or in a sudden strike inshore
Makes off with the pup of an elephant seal,
By every right, his meal;
It's a world of lethal competition

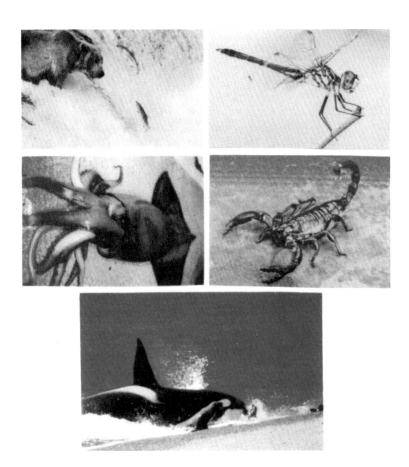

1. Brown bear catching salmon on waterfall, Alaska (p.5).
2. Blue dasher dragonfly (cf. Emperor, p.13).
3. Humboldt Squid on fishing boat (p.5).
4. Scorpion (p.12).
5. Killer whale (*Orcinus orca*) hunting sealion pup (p.2).

6. Young Barn Owl (*Tytos alba*), (p.1).
7. Sea turtles (*Chelonia mydas*), also known as green turtles, coming ashore in Hawaii (p.6).
8. Blacktip reef shark (*Carchahinus melanopterus*), Fiji (p.8).

In the jostling and the fighting for position,
From the microscopic to the gigantic,
From bacteria to the whale,
Hunting, catching,
Raiding, snatching,
In the urgency of hunger
And the fight for the feeding of the young.

Alaskan dawn:
Fighting the stream,
Tails beat and thrash;
The salmon must spawn
Where eagles watch
To make a catch,
And bears are salivating for their fish.

In the sea of Cortes, rising at night,
From the depths where it diligently procreates,
Proliferates, procreates, proliferates,
With full parental anonymity,
Iridescent,
Omnipresent,
Bioluminescent,
Comes the Humboldt Squid with eyes like eggs,
Tentacles instead of fins or legs,
Each with two thousand sucker lips,
Three dozen teeth and a mouth that grips.
Omnivorous, it hunts in mobs;
Anything that moves, it grabs:
Groupers, angel-fish, whatever it can find,
Or when it fancies, one of its own kind.
Swimmers aspire to emulate its skill,
But *whoosh!* it leaves them standing still.

You saw that jellyfish, pushing past smoothly?
Now the sea anemone devours him, patiently.

In the Menai Straits, on patrol in the lustrous water,
Like a robot with some alien operator,
The king-size crab crawls stiffly, with evident hunger,
Each waving pincer
On its remote-controlled arm warning
Of menace and danger,
Till in the boundless mussel-bed, the fertile field,
There's no more waving; the side-stepping predator
Lowers and levers his claw like a JCB digger
And pokes and prods the selfish shellfish
But fails to get his reward.
No matter: this or that mollusc must yield.

As the starfish knows.
You can love your victim to death.
Like this. Go slow.
Embrace. But never let go.
Wrap around. Grip tight.
Clasp your mussel or your whelk
With all your might.
And suck the amorphous life-form out
Into your stomach.
Then,
Discard the useless, empty shell.

They paddle at ease, in a plodding kind of way,
Contented in their shells? No one can say,
Buoyant in their element,
Riding the ripples and the lesser waves,
A bobbing flotilla in the twilight,
A visitation from the waterworld
In urgent need of land.
Seamanship is their heritage.

Who needs a sextant, compass or a satellite
To navigate? Their clumsy body is their instrument,
Their inner compass takes them there,
Directions in their DNA.
Landfall: like fishing-boats broaching the shoreline,
Then humping and heaving out of the spray,
Ungainly in transition, sliding onto the sluggish beach,
Almost, you might think, like a tribe of world-travellers,
Backpackers, ready to camp out all night,
Or a fleet of landing-craft, bent on invasion;
But these are the sea-turtles at their *rendezvous,*
Deliberate amphibians, slow-moving reptiles,
Not intending to stay.
The same beach, says the atavistic memory,
The best beach, the *déja vu* beach,
With superior sand, fit for purpose,
The beach of ancient origin.
Labour of hurried excavation;
Scraping, gouging, no time to lose;
Short legs make poor shovels, but enough.
And now, in the privacy and protection of the night,
In the first or final quarter of the moon,
The *embarazadas* in their sisterhood,
In their mystical and tearful parturition,
The giving of a hundred white and precious eggs,
Receive a brief and glistening satisfaction;
Then give a flailing sand-burial
And a quick farewell.

And all in good hatching-time, not too soon,
See the stirrings in the sand, almost imperceptible:
Something alive, kicking, fighting to find light,
Then all along the shore, life arising, life surprising:
As though a litter of fallen forest-leaves
Had suddenly acquired mobility,
Countless hatchlings, almond-size,

Suddenly on the move,
Wildly waving little flipper-legs,
Scurrying and tumbling in their agitation,
Their mission and intention
To retroject themselves and launch themselves
In a *sauve-qui-peut* precipitation
Into their own home, their bobbing waterworld,
And to follow such direction
As their inner compass takes them.
But a rabble of seabirds are watching, wheeling, screaming;
The gannets have been here before,
Hungry for diving and snatching;
This is their favourite shore;
And there's an irregular army of rock-crabs advancing,
Stiffly, robotically,
Long-arm multi-purpose pincers waving,
Intent on dismembering
Anything helpless and moving,
As if to say, this is our feeding-time.
Yet the sea will welcome any survivors;
Just as each wave falls and reaches its tide-mark,
So it will carry them out on the receding wave
To where the wind will catch them,
Blown to and fro like miniature cobles
With a wild waving of oars, without anchors,
Prey for the superfish, the oceanic predators;
And all along the barrier reef,
Attuned to every movement, every shifting shadow,
The tiger shark glides, patrolling,
Claiming precedence
With high-fish-performance,
Dynamic tail-punch propulsion,
The biggest jaws and sharpest teeth,
As deadly as a sinister submarine
And faster.
Look up, there's a shadow above:

A frenzied waggling on the sea-surface;
One thrust of his mighty tail and he's there,
Nipping the little baby turtle by the flipper;
Next move, to crack the carapace:
A twist, and he has it in his nutcracker jaws,
Crunching and munching the baby shell:
A morsel, not a meal,
And instantly forgotten;
Submerging once again,
He glides among the glowing corals,
Hunting for a more substantial feast.

Downwind,
The jaguar is stalking; now holds still.
Wide-eyed, the young gazelle,
With legs as thin as slender twigs,
Stands listening,
Only ears moving,
Stopped in her tracks,
Two bundles of nerves
Each at the end of an electrified invisible tightrope,
All senses tuned
Until
She turns, she looks away -
A spring, a dash, a brief pursuit
And with a mighty bound
He makes his kill.

And this is the cheetah,
The solitary hunter,
Weaving the veldt, scenting impala there.
With cubs to feed,
She spies and fixes on the weakest of the herd,
Then suddenly transforms into a machine,
Eyes laser-focused, body brain-directed,
Moving in slowest of slow motion

Undetected,
She conceives a tactical surprise,
Uncoils -
With racing swerve and elongated stride,
Flowing like water over a riverbed,
Accelerating into her unchallengeable sprint,
Unconscious of wrath,
With claws unsheathed,
She takes off,
And launches into mid-air,
For an instant ceasing to be herself,
Becoming the messenger of death,
A living missile, hurtling
Headfirst onto her prey,
Clamping its neck with her teeth,
Clawing the strangely unresisting body earthwards;
And the impala, wrong-footed, must fall,
Spindly legs splaying uselessly
In a whirlwind of dust.
Today the cheetah clubs will have their meat.

Watch how the hungry pack of wolves
Pursue the fleeing caribou,
Dividing the herd
And snatching the new-born calves.

Here's a behemoth whose monstrous dominance
Proclaims his unassailability:
The high and mighty elephant,
Trumpeting and bellowing in the distance,
Lumbering through the bush
Like a runaway steamroller,
And toppling trees without permission.
And we respect him
Even when we use him.
Yet there's a flaw in his defence:

He cannot see behind him.
The pride of lions at his back
Find ways to down him.
He sways, as when a mighty tree is felled
And falls at first slowly,
Then topples like a tower in an earthquake;
And then they eat him
With communal flesh-tearing and pawing.
Now he is nothing but meat and bones for gnawing.

The crocodile lies in ambush at the waterhole.
Beware the log that's half-submerged,
Cunningly camouflaged,
Waiting immobile at the water's edge,
Watching with those bulbous, heavily-lidded eyes
The wildebeest that slithers down the bank to drink.
The prey that hesitates is lost;
He steps into a trap;
Those jagged jaws spring wide and snap;
With a wild flailing of its armoured tail
It rolls and drags the struggling victim down
Where the cold dark waters close
And the victim will drown.
I think of prison gates,
Massive, impassive,
Slamming on a prisoner of injustice,
Gripping him in a system that will destroy him
With unconcern.

But now, above, the unaffected herd moves on,
Like a huge frayed carpet animated in the wind,
Raggedly surging, gathering momentum,
Taking the old trail with the old motivation,
Seeking fresh grazing in the Serengeti;
And now they plunge in vast disorder
Into the turbulent Mara

Where hyenas and jackals come circling,
Hungry for their prey,
Exhausted with waiting,
Panting in anticipation,
And who will notice the victims
Lost in migration?

The monkeys come screaming and seeking affray,
But chattering chimpanzees will not be beaten;
Superior intelligence comes into play;
The winners take all: the losers are eaten.

The tamandua claws the termites' nest,
Sniffing, snuffling, probing with his snout;
His barbed and sticky tongue shoots out;
He takes his fill, and comes back later for the rest.

The scorpion stings the fluttering moth.
Poor moth! Consumed not once, but twice.
When scorpion number one had eaten you,
To his surprise,
He was consumed by scorpion number two.

Enough! Hunger forbids mourning.
Life is for living, but also for leaving.

The quick-tongued toad
Patrols the beach at night for food;
Sandhoppers are twitching, jumping, flipping;
So catch them while they're skipping!

The cricket comes to unexpected harm,
Trapped and glued by the velvet worm.

Men do what they're paid for,
Insects, what they're made for.

This morning hatched
On some bearded reed
Or slimy weed
An elegant Aeschna;
Stretched,
Unsticked and unpacked
His crumpled wings, deliberately,
With his own blood pumping up the veins,
A miracle of micro-surgery,
Slowly, finally,
Extending those delicate blades to dry,
Preformed to perfection,
A genius of micro-aviation,
Achieving instant lift-off,
Already knowing how to fly,
Careering round the pond
And zooming through my garden where,
As if propelled by some tiny invisible electric motor
He annexes my air-
Space,
Almost brushing my face;
I stare, get up from my deckchair, to give chase;
And the Emperor Dragonfly hovers
For a micro-moment,
Hovers over my head
In the waft of an imperceptible breeze
With a flicker and flash of his courtly robes,
With his uppermost green and his nethermost blue;
Then speeds over the hedge, too fast to follow;
Eons reinvented in one day;
He performs his role-play
Without question,
Ignoring human players in the action,
Autocratic insect,
Too busy to bask in my admiration .
Of those gauzy, fine-bladed wings,

Faintly tinted like old glass in a church window
I know, or like thin ice melting.
For he is a public service predator,
He needs no instruction;
He flies on a dual mission,
To mate on the wing
And, appetite-driven,
To gobble up gnats
And murder the last mosquito.
He adorns a niche, his special place,
A world without the human race.

And my blackbird will never sing again.
When I bury a bird,
Cat kill or road kill,
I do it with solemnity,
And mark each grave with a cross.

We peer at our birds from within this wooden hide.

Whether they swim in pods or shoals,
Or fly in flocks or congregate in herds,
Whether their domain is air, land or sea,
Whether they slither or crawl,
And whether nature has tailored them with fins and tails
Or wings and talons and claws,
Endowed them with antennae
Or alien appendages,
Painted them in rainbow colours
Or clothed them in drab disguise;
Whether according to their species
They perform balletic rituals and mating dances
Or copulate without affection,
Whether they live for days or years, for seconds or hours,
They have their needs, they have their languages,
That are not ours.

Part II:
In cities and towns

It will come,
Humanity must perforce prey upon itself,
Like monsters of the deep.

King Lear, Act IV, Scene II

(Reading from left to right, top):

9. Peter Sutcliffe (aka The Yorkshire Ripper) in police custody (1983), Express Newspapers. (See p.17).
10. Dr Harold Shipman. (See p.19 and Notes, p.147).
11. Myra Hindley (painting by Marcus Harvey, exhibited at the Royal Academy of Arts, 1997).
12. Ian Brady (1966). (See p.19 and Notes, p.148).
13. Police cease search for Moors victim Keith Bennett, 1 July 2009, Greater Manchester Police handout. (See p.19 as above).
14. London Road, Ipswich, ref. Steve Wright. (See p.26 and Notes, p.154).

Thirteen women.
West Yorkshire folk have not forgotten
How a lorry-driver from Bradford,
A night stalker,
A serial killer,
Was interviewed, repeatedly,
Long before he was apprehended,
And the police had a description,
And a photofit,
While he continued his campaign
Persistently
Till he had murdered thirteen women,
Or more,
Claiming he was *on a mission.*
And he was arrested only by chance.

One boy. Fourteen men.
What better position
To escape recognition,
Deflecting suspicion,
Than working from an information desk,
A civil servant in a JobCentre,
Smiling at strangers:
Can I help ?
(So easy to meet
Unemployables off the street);
Professionally quick
To spot anyone down on his luck;
To check out a no-hoper,
To select a suitable loner
Unaware of the danger,
And invite him home.
These drop-outs would never be missed,
In his five-year campaign
In Willesden, North London:

'What I did had to be done'.
He disposed of the bodies by burning;
'There was no stopping me.'
And when the boy, his first, half-strangled,
Had somehow revived,
And almost survived,
He kept him,
For he was lonely,
And needed company.
In court, the 'Not guilty' plea
Was heard with incredulity.
Sentenced for life, he kept his cool composure,
Listening impassively.

And there lived a couple in Gloucester.
He was an odd-jobbing builder,
And she looked after his children,
And they shared a deficit of empathy,
A personality disorder.
They were malignant, and two of a kind.
When they were apprehended,
And found guilty of their first abduction,
The sentence of the Court
Was moderately kind,
And they were fined
Just £25.
And later,
When they took someone in as a lodger,
Or offered their hospitality
To a trusting stranger,
Their cellar became a torture-chamber,
And their guests were made to disappear.
He was the controlling partner
Till 'Things were getting out of hand'.
He controlled his own death:
He slipped a noose around his neck

And he left her, left her
To face ten counts of murder.
Be glad their house of horror
Has ceased to be inhabited;
It may no longer be visited
By the morbid and curious,
Demolished by order.

And in the Market Street in Hyde,
A family doctor, much respected,
Lethally injected
His patients, undetected;
In his practice, the epitome
Of professional concern and sympathy;
Yet in his soul, deficient in empathy.
No one knows how many died.

Two predatory clerks in Manchester
Indulged their lust
For power and possession,
And preyed on children's trust.
Deficient in emotion,
He was ever the manipulator,
She the willing collaborator;
And they offered no reason
Why on Saddleworth Moor they gave
Each boy or girl a shallow grave.

Hail a taxi, name a destination,
Trust the driver in your expectation
To be taken
Safely, on your journey there.
That's why you pay your fare.
But if a trusting female passenger
Hailed a certain London taxi-driver,
Unknowingly

She faced a monster in his lair
And travelled at a fearful cost.
For twelve long years he preyed successfully
Before arrest.

Did you hear of the minicab driver
Who moonlighted as a burglar
In South London,
With a preference for elderly women
Living alone?
With two hundred offences ascribed to him,
And maybe four hundred more ?
One day in his monstrous career
When his car had been spotted,
He might have been arrested
When a policeman knocked at his door,
But the suspect was said to be 'Not at home',
And the questioning ended there.
Caught in his career
In the seventeenth year,
He earned twentynine verdicts of 'Guilty',
And Scotland Yard made a public apology,
You may think, deservedly.

The schoolgirl's unforgettable face
Materialised like a ghost
On the TV screen, as if still lost,
And still appealing to be found, though
Last seen living nineteen years ago.
Strathclyde Police had failed;
The case went cold.
Her mother lost the will to live
And died distraught.
The missing schoolgirl's sister bore the pain
For seventeen years, until
In Margate and in Bathgate

And all the killer's houses of concealment,
A systematic excavation
And a shocking exhumation
Exposed the evidence where it had lain.
And with the closure, and the killer caught,
The schoolgirl's sister, now a mother,
Found the cloud was lifted;
And her children gave her hope again.
In Margate and in Bathgate,
And all the killer's houses of concealment,
Undetected,
The evidence had lain.

Released for just one hour
In Tooting, London,
A proven danger to the public,
A paranoid schizophrenic
Absconded.
This stabbing was his latest.
His victim, a passing cyclist,
Who fell, mortally wounded,
In Tooting, London.

And another prisoner on release,
Untouched by rehabilitation,
Took a hammer to the harmless:
A mother, defenceless,
With her little daughter,
In her innocence;
His mindless violence
Appalled the nation.
The mother died.
Somehow, alone,
The little girl survived.

Early release for one obsessive prisoner
Meant terror for his former partner.
She was his victim, but she had no choice.
She was his victim twice over:
This time he killed her.

Or you may have heard of the prisoner
Banged up for stabbing his former partner,
Who nearly lost her life.
Then, on release, in Tamworth,
This former prisoner killed his wife.

And there are predators more subtle yet,
Plausible masters
And monsters of the internet.
He was a known offender
In Teesdale, Tyne and Wear,
Who had seen a girl's face
And stalked her in cyberspace.
He had found her online,
Too innocent for fear;
He kidnapped her and murdered her,
In Teesdale, Tyne and Wear.
.

In the Midlands, you may have heard
Of a respected citizen
Who had fathered four children
And enhanced his reputation,
For he was no fool,
Wearing the well-pressed suit of Education
By serving at a school
On the Governing Board.
This family man, with four children,
Preyed on women and young girls
As if life were no more than a game of bowls
And they the skittles,

Escaping detection with plausible lies
And neat alibis
For twenty six years.

And there lived another good citizen,
An Austrian, in Amstetten,
A family man so strict
At the table, and so correct,
You would never connect
Him with deception;
Meticulous in all things mechanical,
But in his family life, tyrannical;
No doubting his ability;
His cover-up, a masterpiece of plausibility.
In engineering he was multiskilled.
He practised both design and build.
This master-constructor
And cunning abductor
Devised a cellar
Where he imprisoned his own daughter
For fourteen long years;
He fathered seven children by her,
Insisting he was 'not a monster'.

And another Austrian abductor
Snatched a schoolgirl when she was only ten,
Enslaved her, and took her for his paramour.
In a run-down suburb of Vienna
He kept her as his prisoner
For eight long years
In a secret cellar.
Till one day,
His vigilance astray,
She ran away.
When he committed suicide
She cried.

Today she lives alone, and in her mind
Is still confined.

In Ryazan, in Russia,
Two girls were concealed in a cellar
By their abductor.
As they said when they told of their terror,
'In the dark and the cold,
It was like the end of the world.'
It was only their companionship
For four long years
That kept their hope alive.
Discovered by police
They said on their release,
'You should never allow yourself
To become a victim.'
Today they lead a normal life.

In a small town called Antioch,
In North Carolina, near San Francisco,
Lived a raptor and repeat offender,
Considered 'creepy' by his neighbour.
With a fifty-year sentence
For his first offence,
He was released after only ten.
He was 'On probation',
Under superficial supervision.
Now he stole someone else's daughter
While she waited for the bus to go to school.
And she was only eleven,
And she lived in Nevada
Near Lake Tahoe,
Like his first victim.
But he took her and imprisoned her, sixty miles away,
While her friends lit candles and prayed for her.
'There was a summer of fear in Tahoe'.

And he had two children by her.
And they adored him as their father
For eighteen long years.
Later she said, 'He stole my life.'
Though reported by his neighbour,
He kept all three prisoner
Behind a tall fence in his garden,
Behind the foliage of his thickly planted garden.
He received three life sentences,
And in court he claimed to be guided by God.

In Cleveland, Ohio,
Two girls went missing from the same street.
Searches took place without success
And a vigil was held, with prayers and candles.
And one of the searchers,
Who made a donation,
And took part in the vigil,
Had driven a school bus for twentytwo years,
And he was a musician,
An immigrant, born in Puerto Rico,
Friendly, amenable, beyond suspicion.
His house was mainly boarded up,
A run-down, shabby property;
But that was his own business;
He rarely had visitors,
And supervised admission.
It was ten long years since the girls had gone missing.
And the mystery remained,
Their disappearance unexplained,
When one day, at an attic window,
Appeared a girl's face,
The face of a six-year-old girl,
And it made no sense.

The neighbours knocked at his door;

A commotion inside:
From within a girl cried,
Desperately begging for help
While the owner was out.
The rest was a gift for the press;
For this callous offence
The judge gave a sentence for life,
And a thousand years,
But the kidnapper served rather less;
With calm indifference
And absence of remorse,
He contrived his own death.

Now call to mind the night-time cruiser,
In an Eastern town, a fork-lift truck driver,
Switching roles like a real-life actor,
Hating the world that denied him
Whatever he wanted and hoped for.
Here he comes again in his car, cruising,
Looming out of the netherworld at night,
In the redlight district near the football ground
In an Eastern town. where the working girls stand,
Waiting for a client on the London Road.
A working girl walks the cliff-edge of danger:
She quips, 'Haven't I seen you before ?'
But when he slams the door behind her
She dances to death with a strangler.
And when, after this killer has taken five lives,
And terrorised an Eastern town,
He is caught, and questions are asked,
He will say only, 'No comment',
Only, 'No comment',
'No comment', 'No comment',
And 'No comment'.

Nor could I ever explain
How, in the East End of London,
Capital of Empire,
More than a century ago,
The murder and mutilation
Of Whitechapel working-class women
Escaped detection,
Or how the mystery could inspire
For writers, researchers and readers of fiction
An odd allure
And a wretched fascination.

Part III:
In human conflict

Man's inhumanity to man
makes thousands mourn.

Man Was Made to Mourn, Robert Burns

Wahn! Wahn! Überall Wahn!

*Hans Sachs, in Act III of Die Meistersinger
von Nürnberg,* Richard Wagner

Alexander

Look back on Thebes in flames
When thousands lost their lives
To make an Alexander Great;
No monument records their names
And no memorial survives
To honour those whose flesh his fires consumed.

15. Alexander depicted as the son of the god Amun, the Egyptian king of the gods. (Obverse of a silver tetradrachm of Lysimachus, formerly one of Alexander's officers, who succeeded Alexander and became King of Thrace, Asia Minor and Macedonia in 306 BC).

The Massacre of the Innocents

Remember how King Herod the Great
Had murdered a wife and two sons
With never an inkling of remorse,
Revelling in a deficit of empathy
And an appetite for executions?
But that was once upon a time;
He rests his notoriety upon another crime;
A painter brings these executions up to date.

Herod gave the order,
But not as in Scripture
And not when the Gospel ascribes it.
Pieter Brueghel the Elder
With licensed updating
And thoughtful relocating
Revisits and describes it
As a Netherlandish massacre
In a Netherlandish winter.

Brueghel has the measure of your comfort zone,
Your instinct for self-preservation,
Your distancing, your denial,
Permitting you to turn away;
He accepts your rights as spectator,
As is proper;
No, you were not responsible;
That was then, this is today.

Both the frozen-hearted perpetrator
Painted at the apex of the picture,
And his distant royal master,
King Philip the Second, the controller,
The Spanish Empire micro-manager,
Are gone forever;
Their only court appearance
Rests upon this page, posthumously,
And in the painter's vision for posterity,
In the whiteness of winter.
Witness a scene of calculated violence:
At work in the middle-ground, left of centre,
A hard man, one of the henchmen,
In a cruelty worthy of Bosch,
Has wrenched a little child from its mother
And swings it by one arm,
As if swinging a bird by its wing,
While the mother collapses, weeping.
In the foreground right,
The heavies have moved in;
For they provide the dynamic;
And they're warming to their work,
To search out and kill;
They scent and pursue their human prey
With the vigour and intent of huntsmen;
For this is no sport,
And the panic is visible,
The terror is tangible;
And no one is safe amid the carnage
As proof of their skill
In fishing out children in hiding
For the quick despatch of stabbing and throat-cutting.

Composed in the right of centre
Sits the Herald on horseback,
Above it all, as if to say,

To the menfolk begging for mercy,
'I bring you this message
In the name of the great and excellent ruler
Of this miserable realm, by the Grace of God,
Protector of Peace
And Bringer of Justice,
His Supreme Highness King Philip of Spain,
In whose presence your worthlessness
Would render you unfit even to grovel with the dogs
That crawl for scraps beneath his table,
That you, the base inhabitants of this wretched village
Must surrender your bawling infants and babies,
Expecting no redress;

And should anyone resist his Majesty's command
On the rightful instructions of his loyal appointed officers,
He will die;
For we are only obeying orders
From on high.
So keep your filthy hands off me, and let me pass.'

While all across the village street
Awhirl with seizings, grapplings,
Grabbings, brute-force pushings and shovings,
Haulings out, hard knocks and snatchings,
The henchmen and hitmen of the Duke
Destroy a generation,
To the wild barking of every village dog,
Every dog barking,
Wildly, barking at strangers,
All in a world of two dimensions,
Arrested,
Motionless,
In a tableau never to be animated,
Like a motion picture
Frozen forever on a single frame,

The screaming hurly-burly redoubled
By the stillness and silence,
By the fierce imminence
Of its ready-to-burst explosiveness.
While in the background, in the centre,
At the apex of this composition,
Clothed all in black,
Black against the winter-whiteness,
Watching, controlling,
With the long beard of authority,
Heading a troop of mounted soldiers in formation,
With lances aloft
And ready if need be to obey any order,
There sits the appointed Governor
Of this miserable province,
Despot-appointed despot,
Delegate of absolute power,
Tyrant in this hate-filled foreign land,
Watching, waiting,
The Duke of Alva.

A lesson and an illustration
From the text-book of repression:
A Netherlandish massacre
In a Netherlandish winter.

Jerusalem: The First Crusade

Urban II

Dieu le Volt!
Divine Imperative!
I woke, I breathed, I knew.
I do not recollect
The whirlwind of a revelation
Or lightning flash
Or sudden stunning thunderbolt
Splitting the dome of heaven,
Shedding the golden radiance of the divine,
Seeking me, choosing me,
Calling me by name
In some mysterious visitation
For heavenly purposes,
By preference or favour
Barely earned,
Or whether God laid constant siege to my soul,
Battering the gate of my heart,
Investing my affections,
Eager to take the citadel of my sinful self
With a well-aimed holy trebuchet.
No, it was not like that.
I always knew that I was blest;
Conviction grew, but I felt no touch,
No otherworldly intervention,
No Damascene epiphany.
I was myself a work in progress

Because I had work to do,
As in pruning the overgrown tree;
Cutting out the deadwood,
Lifting the curse of simony,
Restructuring, delivering order;
My mission, above all, to reclaim
The rights of the pontificate,
Rebuilding all the pillars of authority
Whereby our Mother Church sustains
The one true Catholic faith;
I needed no conversion;
The inner voice that brings me to my knees
For penance and reflection,
The voice that calms, and sprinkles love
Like a gentle shower on a summer's day,
That cleanses the soul of every evil intention,
Planting and watering the seeds of peace,
Is fatherly, and seems familiar,
Transmitting messages from one who went before me,
His mission, to assure me;
I follow in the footsteps of Gregorius,
Who prophesied, and smote the infidels;
I listen daily to his voice, and heed;
For he who must lead
Must be guided by his own true vision;
When others ask for spiritual direction,
I am the oracle, and I say also this:
'Come with me to Italy;
I prophesy a seat of power in Rome'.

Sometimes I hear that voice
When tramping on a pilgrimage,
Or fasting, in a time of penitence;
It speaks in tones accustomed to obedience
And in a forthright manner you can trust,
Uttering injunctions that you must

Obey,
Such as an urgent call to arms,
Not crafted in some indecipherable code
Or misted in Delphic ambiguity,
But resonating like a monastery bell,
Recasting its deafening bellstrokes into words
Like molten metal tipped into a mould,
In liquid fire from the furnace of Creation.
It speaks the living language of today,
Yours and mine,
As in the mystic voice that cleansed the ear
Of Moses on the mountaintop,
Delivering the Decalogue,
The ineradicable and universal Law,
Blinding in its clarity,
Binding in its authority:
This voice has called for Holy War.
And there can be no man living, breathing,
Walking closer to his Maker,
Than the Holy Father,
God's mouthpiece and interpreter;
No man better qualified,
And some say pre-ordained,
To pray 'Thy Kingdom come!'
And one who knows that war is just
When war advances Christendom;
And every Christian sword
No matter with whose blood
It may be stained, is blest
And sanctified,
When wielded by a Christian warrior,
To liberate Jerusalem:
The Holy Sepulchre must be liberated!
(I hear the sound of thunder in my head).
A priestly paradox, no doubt,
That slaughter may be pleasing unto God!

Alexius I

Cautious, yet ambitious,
The Emperor Alexius
Indulged each day in day-dreams
And woke each night from night-dreams
Of patching up his Empire in the East.
Byzantium itself was under threat.
Precious Antioch was lost,
Besieged and taken by the Turks,
Likewise Nicaea, where money spoke louder than words,
Where merchants and dealers grew fat
And ate from platters made from beaten gold,
Where ancient councils met
And wise men took their cue from Constantine,
Whose brilliant masterstroke
Made Christians into soldiers
And Church the grateful subject of his patronage,
Beholden to the Emperor.
(May fortune never leave the Emperor
Beholden to the Pope !)

The East, Alexius groaned, was his by right,
His fast-diminishing inheritance;
And further still, like the tempting fruit
On the tallest pomegranate tree,
Beyond his itching grasp,
The fabled prize for every infidel invader,
The Holy City of Jerusalem.
For, rooted in the fertile brain
Of cautious, yet ambitious
Emperor Alexius,
Lay the tender seedling of a plan
Whose nursing to fruition.
Had he the means of execution,
Would secure the *summum bonum*,

The capture of Jerusalem
With the golden glory of its temple;
Jerusalem, the centre of the world,
Best market for all trade;
Secure the subjugation
Of its diverse population;
Muslims, Christians, Turks and Jews;
Fat merchants and lean camel-dealers,
Silk purveyors and spice-traders,
Middle-men and stony-hearted money-lenders,
Private militias and mercenaries,
Horse-thieves and street-beggars,
Babbling idiots and raving zealots,
And their assimilation
By Imperial decree
Into a limitless Empire
Worthy of a new Alexander,
With rich potential for taxation,
Tribute and rare treasure
To add to his collection;
Untold impediments lay before him
As vast as the desert, and as intractable;
Therefore let others do the work for him,
Let them deliver to Byzantium
The Holy City of Jerusalem.

Alexius dreamed, and drank, and dreamed again:
Conjectured an alliance
Of profit and convenience
With one whose spiritual power
Could match his own authority,
His counterpart and *alter ego* in the West,
Whose calling and anointed eminence
Ensured that every uttered word
Was sanctified and heard
With solemn deference.

For all agree, the spiritual and temporal
May walk on earth in perfect parallel;
Should they desire to meet,
Each may walk the same mosaic floor
In villa, palace or temple,
And eat at the same table -
Though each prefers to drink
From his own cup.
Great men may think alike
But do not always drink alike.
They may conceive a common plan
With separate interests,
Each with an eye to his own advantage,
But sympathetic partners in collusion.

And so, with guesswork or foreknowledge,
Alexius cast his diplomatic net:
His envoy made his pitch at Piacenza,
Where the Papal Council met,
Requesting military aid;
And later that same year, in Southern France,
At Clermont, in the Pope's own voice,
The Emperor's request was heard again,
Adopted in a passionate campaign:
Urban the Second, with all his eloquence,
And driven by his admirable ambition
To unify divided Christendom,
Delivered an inflammatory sermon:
A call to arms to liberate Jerusalem
And rescue Christians from atrocities
Committed by the infidels,
But most of all to end
The desecration of the Holy Sepulchre.
The Pope became the message
And his theme adopted him,
Played well to sundry audiences

On tour in every town and village,
Repeated and embroidered,
Talked up to wide-eyed countrymen,
Masters and servants, knights and retainers,
With hellish and horrific instances
Designed to stir up calls for retribution;
It takes atrocities to justify atrocities;
His speech with all its rhetoric erupted
Like Vesuvius, with bloody consequences,
All in the name of God;
It was a speech that travelled well,
Assumed a life of its own,
Found legs and walked and talked,
Recruited Princes, warlords, commoners,
And in its clever naming of the enemy
Unblocked a pyroclastic flow of indignation
To redirect the warlords from their fruitless feuds
And motivate the holy expedition.
Dieu le volt.

One more nightmare for Alexius.
He who rules Byzantium controls the Bosphorus.
Weary and hungry crusaders collect at his gates
In straggling columns, irregular cohorts,
All sorts and conditions of men, armed and unarmed,
From Frankish princes riding their fine horses
And knights and retainers on capable mounts
And warriors with swords, bows and lances,
To footsore servants and loyal retainers
And strings of camp-followers,
Drunk and disorderly ne'er-do-wells,
Dispensing a medley of jests and oaths,
Often in strange languages.
With a show of making all welcome,
The Emperor's hospitality flows
With meat and drink for the Frankish princes;

But his officers are under instruction:
One overnight camp for each contingent,
While Bohemond pays the sea-captains,
Before the pressing business of embarcation
And a choppy, unsteady sea-passage
To ferry them safely over the Bosphorus.
Meanwhile, to the princes of evident wealth,
Conspicuous in status and authority,
Alexius will extend a gracious hand;
Each prince must be impressed, with wine,
A little flattery, a touch of conviviality,
And the honour of an invitation
To a private audience with the Emperor
In the Palace of the Blachernae.
Each guest will be guided, one by one,
By the fair-haired inscrutable captains
Of the Emperor's fearsome Varengian Guard
Through marble colonnades
And quiet courtyards open to the sky,
Where fountains jet, and sprinkle guests
And passers by;
And arcs of water, intermittently,
Sparkle in the sunlight, or spout
From the mouths of fabulous beasts;
Each Frankish prince in turn will pass
Through the shade of a cool ante-room
Where a leopard on its chain sits watching,
Close to a golden gryphon, ingenious automaton,
That nods, extends its seeming-hungry beak,
And opens and retracts its lion claws;
And here the guest delivers up his sword,
Before a guard unlocks the golden doors,
To gain admittance to the lofty presence
Of one whose wealth and power and dignity
Will rightly humble and intimidate;
Each prince must pay obeisance to the Emperor.

Each prince, and for himself alone, must bow
And swear upon his vestment's Holy Cross
A declaration of allegiance to the Emperor
And promise to transfer to him
All titles of all conquests, howsoever won.

As *quid pro quo*, the Emperor will be pleased
To lend the expedition his support;
With what supplies, how many troops, how far away,
And when, he does not say.
Raymond, whose princely reputation
 Has guaranteed a pass, declines to play a part
In this dishonourable exercise.
Handsome Bohemond has bowed his head;
Alexius knows this man's military skill;
Seeking to buy the Italian Norman's loyalty,
He treats him like a favourite son,
Showering him with gold and glittering gifts;
Bohemond swears an oath he will not keep,
For in the turmoil of a bitter siege
He will abandon this campaign
Intemperately, temporarily,
For his own gain;
His nephew Tancred bridles at the thought
Of soft submission or subservience;
He will not swear allegiance to any man,
Even in the palace and imperial presence
Of this all-controlling potentate;
He hates a show of menial deference
And slips away with all his knights
Across the windy Bosphorus,
To join the swarming vast assembly
Of these contrary contingents,
Their leaders incompatible,
With the shouting and the swearing and the singing
And the babel and fervour and confusion

And hysteria and excitement
Of this divided yet united
And unlikely expedition.

The Long March

Others have marshalled all the military facts:
Towns and villages taken and looted,
Tally of enemies killed;
Numbers of knights, horsemen, foot soldiers, archers,
Armourers, blacksmiths, cooks and camp-followers,
From princes to peasants in feudal demarcation,
Encouraged, chastened and exhorted
By a cohort of priests, loudly praising God;
Called into an alliance of feudal militias
Conjoined under jealous commanders,
Knitted together by a fine invisible membrane
Of faith, as battleproof as chainmail;
An assortment of religious adventurers,
A *bouillabaisse* of an army.

Others have told how the expedition stumbled
And faltered on the long march south,
In an *impasse* of sieges and skirmishes,
Turkish attacks and counter-attacks,
Blockaded in a counter-siege, exhausted
In a two-year trauma of inconclusive engagements;
A tale of dissension and disputes between leaders,
And shortage of supplies, and thirst and starvation,
And sickness, and attrition from disease;
 How some died from dehydration,
 Collapsing in the desert heat
 With wounds unhealed by prayer or incantation
Or, falling under the spell of some hallucination
Would rave and babble unintelligibly,
Till Peter Bartholomew, as in a trance,

Announced his finding of *The Holy Lance*
And rescued and restored the expedition.
Others have unfolded on the page
With greater diligence and acumen
The holy pageant of disasters.
This narrative will overleap the past,
And take the desert road to come at last
Towards the final reckoning.

The weakest had fallen. So had the bravest,
Culled by the constant invisible Angel of Death
From all that banner-waving multitude
Who in a compact with the Emperor
Had swarmed across the windy Bosphorus
Where East in all its otherness meets West,
And landed like a plague of locusts,
Invaders on an alien shore.

Losses had left their military disposition
Leaner and more fit for purpose:
Soldiers schooled like Spartans in privation,
Each man, leader or follower,
Each knight or priest or commoner,
Most suited to his place and function;

Expect a Crusader, in vanguard or rearguard,
Engineer or armourer, storeman or stableman;
To shake his fist at harsh adversity,
And bury old feuds in *camaraderie*;
But 'right of conquest' still fanned the flames
Of all the Frankish princes' jealousy.

Not marching in phalanx or formation,
But trudging in clusters of comrades-in-arms,
Divided by custom, according to region,
And graded in order of rank and title,

Each man attends his own commander,
Trusting him alone to issue an order.

Jolting on a baggage-horse, his warhorse behind him,
At the head of the column, rides Raymond of St Gilles,
In prime position for the surge through the gates
To take surrender of Jerusalem, and that greater honour,
To repossess the Holy Sepulchre
Defiled and desecrated by the infidels.

His knights and attendants can scarcely keep up with him;
Some have lost their horses, riding on donkeys
Or swaying on handcarts, dazed by the desert heat,
While others fall back, to join the walking wounded,
With the baggage-train and the cooks and capon-cages
And the camp-followers and kitchen-wenches.

Cantering behind the handcarts, keeping his distance,
Comes Godfrey of Bouillon with his Lotharingian knights
And his German warriors, ferocious in the field,
Diminished in number but not in reputation;
Godfrey, born a soldier, born to direct
The fiery breakthrough at the city walls.

Here comes Tancred, new Prince of Bethlehem,
Welcomed, not as a conqueror, but as a friend;
In alliance with Godfrey, and in his retinue,
Leaving his uncle Bohemond at Antioch,
His by right of conquest, and to rule,
And leaving all the Italian Normans behind;
Here comes the most noble, Count Hugh of Vermandois,
The scheming brother to the King of France;
And here comes the most base, Baldwin of Boulogne,
Brother to Godfrey, a byword for greed.
And with him, now under suspicion,
Peter Bartholomew, finder of *The Holy Lance*,

And Robert of Normandy, son of the Conqueror,
Still fronting his army of hawk-eyed archers
Trained by the handful of honoured veterans
Who smote and killed the Anglo-Saxon King;
And Arnulf of Chocques, with his golden cross,
Whose undisputed claims would make him Patriarch.

And at night comes the sound of a minstrel singing,
Always from Raymond's tent, and heard by the sentries,
A fine honeyed voice, an instrument of beauty,
Honoured and favoured by the nobility,
Telling in a vein of enchanting poetry,
In a sweet new sound, a lilting pastourela,

Of a knight who pines to return to his own country.
And Raymond must hear again a song of Roland:
'The morning light is cool and white and clear;
Above the eastern hills there lifts a great flambeau,
Its fire reflected on the point of every spear,
And glowing on the blades of swords and lances.'

Before the march begins, a Latin Mass;
Vexilla Regis is their marching song;
The Benedictine monks walk on, singing; how they love
The sound of the Psalms on the trail through the hills.
Often they cry out, and call on their Saint, to grant
His guidance in this Just and Holy War.

On the hilltop the scouts raise a cross: 'The way is clear!'
In awe, like Israelites before the Promised Land,
Crusaders kneel at first sight of the city walls,
The Dome of the Rock, the mighty battlements;
Parched lips perform a prayer, hoarse voices force a cheer,
And Tancred weeps to see his dream draw near.
Yet when the holy expedition halted
Before those high impenetrable walls,

Accomplished, but with energy depleted,
Hearts sank to contemplate another siege,
And disillusion spread; some few deserted,
And some crusaders died beside the poisoned wells.

The Great Assault

Others may tell the never-ending story
Of Abraham, of David, of the Ark, and of Solomon,
And how this welcoming cosmopolis
Became the spiritual home of Christians,
Muslims, Jews; one God, though still divided;
How Egypt came to rule Jerusalem
And how the Fatimids had manned the towers,
With early warning of these new invaders,
Had taken in supplies and underpinned defences
Against the Western infidels, the mad crusaders.
How they in turn made preparations for attack,
Their hopes buoyed up by new supplies,
Delivered to their nearest port,
Of nails, axes, ropes for the great siege-engines
Essential for the planned assault;
Yet these crusaders in their madness
Day after day disputed who should rule
According to the rubric of God's will.
Dieu le Volt!
When a vision was needed, one man was blest:
The time had come for Peter Desiderius.
The Pope had sent his legate, Bishop Adhémar,
To lead and share the sufferings of his warrior flock,
Now, after great privation, Adhémar was dead,
And with him his divine authority;
But in a vision he appeared,
So Peter said,
With strict instructions for a penitential fast
And a military parade,

A show of strength and unity
To boost morale and terrorise the enemy.
The troops were formed in one prodigious column
To circumambulate the city of Jerusalem;
First in the procession, the barefooted clerics,
Shouldering wooden crosses and waving saintly relics,
Chanting psalms in sonorous Latin;
Behind them, the knights parading in full armour,
In gambesons that bore the red crusader cross,
Lances held aloft with pennants flying;
Next a massed array of Norman archers, well equipped;
And next the footsoldiers, five abreast,
Some blowing trumpets, some emitting cries
As if to split the city walls asunder
And make Jerusalem a Jericho,
And others beating swords on shields
In time with every second step,
And wagons with stones to hurl from trebuchets,
And last, a file of able-bodied men,
Brandishing swords and daggers, axes, pikes and clubs,
All thirsting for action.
Egyptians on the walls were unimpressed;
Some waved their swords in mockery and laughed;
They greeted this parade with incredulity;
Their archers showered arrows from the sky,
And shook their heads in disbelief
To see the column come to rest
Beside the Mount of Olives,
Knights and soldiers gathering loosely round,
In a motley congregation,
To hear the sermons from the chaplains;
Peter the Hermit gave the sermon of his life,
And those who heard it said that it was good.
He ended with a Benediction;
The expedition was enthused, revived,
And came together, as he knew it would.

Christians outside the walls gave good advice.
They knew a source of timber in the hills,
In woodland, bordering Samaria.
It took a hundred men two weary days
To find and fell the trees and trim the logs
And haul the load on wagons to Jerusalem.
And there, with skill and hard-earned expertise,
They laboured to advance the holy cause,
Their faith enshrined in every knot and nail
That fixed and raised the strange construction.
The thump and crack of axes echoed from the walls
As engineers prepared these giants of destruction:
Two great assault-machines, four storeys high,
Mobile and manoeuvrable, with a sturdy roof,
And platforms to take five fighting men abreast,
Yet shielded from the missiles of the enemy.
The cost, three weeks of preparation
Till they were ready for action. Only then
Would these crusaders call for God's protection
And launch the final phase of their campaign.
In a cold dawn, with chilling apprehension,
The Fatimids beheld the weapons for invasion:
Two siege-towers with platforms for attack,
Ladders to support a bold incursion,
And a battering-ram for ultimate persuasion.

But Raymond at the southern wall was thwarted;
His tower, of insufficient height, the target
For every missile that the Fatimids could muster;
They loaded their own mangonels that hurled
Boulders that crashed and caused his tower to sway;
Showers of arrows embedded themselves in shields,
Or penetrated flesh; crusaders' bodies crumpled;
Sheets of Greek fire fell on the struggling invaders,
And seared their exposed skin like meat on a spit,
As firebrands hissed with trails of choking smoke

And smouldered on the tower's hide-protected walls;
Soon Raymond's tower was set alight, and slowly tilted,
Till in a storm of scattering sparks and splinters
It split from side to side and burst apart
As if it loved to feed the glowing flames,
While at St Stephen's Gate the iron-tipped battering-ram,
Heaved forward by a score of able-bodied men,
Had wedged itself immovably
Between the outer and the inner city wall,
There to be set on fire, contested, owned and disowned,
A wrecked contraption and a warning sign
Of human folly and the waste of war.
Tancred, with Godfrey at the northern wall,
Had raised a ladder for an *escalade*;
His foremost warrior fought precariously
Until, most pitifully wounded, forced back;
Determined, Godfrey launched a fierce attack;
His tower had relocated overnight;
In utmost silence and in secrecy,
His able-bodied men and engineers
Had part dismantled, loaded, with much labour,
Wheeled and transported every timber section
Of his waddling, lumbering, warfaring siege-monster
Into a new and ominous position,
And where the city wall was weakly fortified.
He now enjoyed a tactical advantage:
His warriors faced downhill, the Fatimids faced up;
See who could now inflict the greater damage.
On the topmost platform, in full command,
Godfrey shared the danger with his men;
And when his able-bodied team below
Applied the final heave to edge his tower
Almost to arm's length from the city walls,
He caused the hurdle at the top
To drop at once to close the gap;
It fell tight like the lid of a family chest;

By such laborious means and sharp devices
Are battles won and cities overrun;
At once this bridge became a bridgehead;
Invaders surged forward, elbow to elbow,
Eager as a pack of wolves, leaping,
Snarling, falling hungrily on their prey,
Each man eager to be first
To grapple with defenders,
Fighting at close quarters,
In a *mêlée sans pareil,*
Blow by counterblow,
Christians and Muslims locked in combat
Hand to hand
With cries of 'Allah Akbar !'
Mingling with 'Dieu le Volt !'
And panting, pushing,
Slashing, stabbing,
To the sound of screams
As soldiers toppled to their deaths below.
Until there came an almost silent moment,
A frozen struggle and a tipping-point
As sharp as any sword
When weight of numbers
Bore down on the defenders,
And at that moment of transition
From past to altered future,
That subliminary pause or hesitation
When the world would change for ever, -
A nearby turret on the wall caught fire;
The Fatimids gave way,
And turned and fled.
In a defining act,
The Christian warriors seized the day:
Ludolf and Engelbert of Tournai were first
Over the top,
To prove that Godfrey of Bouillon

With his Lotharingian knights
Had won the right of conquest,
The victor's honour and the victor's spoils.

Others have gathered and sifted all the evidence
And coloured in the graphics, unsparingly, in red;
This was a model for all massacres,
Methodical in its mercilessness,
A vengeance visited on every Muslim, every Jew.
'Show them no mercy,
Let there be nowhere to hide,
For God is on our side!'
Survivors flee screaming to the Temple Mount;
The Aqsā mosque will never hold them all,
Mothers clutching babies, dragging crying children,
Jostling, scrambling, desperate for sanctuary;
They huddle against pillars and pack into corners,
In the home and prayer-house of their religion
As though Qur'anic verses hastily chanted
Can save them from the Christian warriors' wrath.

Witness the product of the Pope's imagination,
Inspiring Christians with his blood-boiling sermon
To recreate a hell on earth,
Killers and victims cruelly reversed:
For he and only he
Could speak the mind of God
And make atrocities excuse atrocities;
For Urban's airy dispensation
Had sprouted men absolved from any guilt,
Licensed to kill, and penance-free
From any righteous crime
Committed with a sword in the right hand
And a crucifix in the left;
Crusaders in their righteous faith
Would hold a Festival of Butchery,

Plunging deep into the pit of mayhem
In the slaughterhouse that was Jerusalem.

Raymond

No doubting Godfrey's military·skill;
While in the south, repulsed, despairing,
Count Raymond, groaning in frustration,
Has fallen back to safety at Mount Zion,
His tower a useless, black and smouldering wreck,
Battered by stones from well-aimed mangonels;
The news from Godfrey fills him with chagrin;
His rival's breakthrough on the northern wall
Gained right of conquest and the right to rule;
For Godfrey's leadership and *savoir faire*,
A valiant victory by *force majeure*;
For Raymond, stinging humiliation;
His leadership is called in question;
So much for seniority;
No greater downfall than a failed attack.
He takes a lesson in determination:
'*Aux armes!*' he cries in desperation,
'Bring up the ladder for an *escalade*
And one last brave assault!'
Helmeted and in hauberk, sword swinging in scabbard,
His bravest warrior climbs, surmounts the wall;
Surprised, he gasps: 'The Fatimids have fled !'
But whether their wounds have haemorrhaged their ardour,
Or reports from the North have splintered their resolve,
The Egyptian defenders have jettisoned their arms
And melted away, like ice on a summer's day.
Rarely in battle does a gain come free.
A moment of bewilderment and doubt:
Count Raymond's dream is broken like a lance
Shattered and useless in a tournament.
His deepest wish, to storm the battlements

Wth honour, in a grand assault, to save
The Holy Sepulchre from the infidels,
To rescue relics dear to Christendom,
And his prime ambition, *Deo Volente*,
To rule in peace, with no impediment -
Dismissed and vetoed by Almighty God.
Count Raymond thanks his God for governance,
But overcome and battle-weary, he is sick,
Sick to his soul, in his injured pride.
He owes a penance for his sins,
The mortal sins of pride and jealousy.
He kneels and prays in all humility;
In all our trials, God is on our side.

With every siege there comes the need for closure;
The anguish is over; take heart, the time has come;
And every victory is incomplete
Without the formal business of surrender,
The kneeling in submission,
The recognition of defeat,
The visible deposition
And divestiture of arms and armour;
Godfrey has felled a mighty tree
Whose trunk and branches lie prostrate before him.
Raymond must step into that vacant place,
And in his own unchallengeable right,
Reject the option to negotiate;
He will control the protocol;
He will dictate the terms;
He will hammer out the future;
He owns the diplomatic battlefield.
The Tower of David guards the Jaffa Gate.
The Tower and its curtain wall enclose
The independent fortress citadel,
The military base and garrison;
For Egypt ruled the city from afar;

The garrison commander, Iftikhãr,
Was proven in experience, well prepared,
For any siege, attack, or act of war.
And here he organised his arsenal,
The storehouse, barracks and the treasury,
His operations centre and HQ,
A tight, sustainable establishment.
And here, in flight from Godfrey's victory
The remnants of the city guards withdrew.
While Raymond thanked and glorified his God,
So Iftikhãr prayed to Allah and to Rã.

And Raymond sends a loyal and trusted knight,
With a captive Muslim as interpreter,
As envoy to his Muslim adversary,
Amener à une capitulation
With keys to the tower and the citadel,
And offering, in his magnanimity,
Safe conduct, open to negotiation.
Beside a merchant's house, deserted, plundered,
There stands a cistern with the purest water
Such as his soldiers in the siege had longed for,
When Iftikhãr had poisoned all the wells;
Here with his seneschal, his priest and servants,
Count Raymond drinks, washes, changes garments:
Fresh from the baggage-train, his gambeson;
A hauberk free from dust and mud;
A surcoat, unbloodied, trimmed with gold,
Bearing the cross, itself blood-red;
A dagger in a golden belt around his waist,
And in a scabbard richly chased
He will bear his mighty ceremonial sword,
In its hilt, a costly piece of craftsmanship,
A cross inset with gleaming precious stones.
And he speaks to his seneschal as if to his brother:
'Bring me my greatsword, my godsent Durendal;

If you hold your ear to the hilt, you will hear his voice,
Comversing, advising, singing, humming or hissing;
Durendal, who lives in my handgrip and leads
From the front, in battle, for others to follow;
Protector, defender, oracle, cleanser from evil,
God-blest light-giver, well-tempered companion,
My guide, my strength, my noble Durendal.'
And he speaks to his groom as if to a dear friend:
'Bring me my warhorse, my Veuillantil;
My purpose is to awe and overpower;
I need to show these rank Egyptians
That the Christian warrior is invincible'.
'You look thinner, bonier now, Veuillantil;
Come to me, let me whisper in your ear.
Together we pursued the shimmering, glittering,
Thirst-arousing, promise-cheating,
Ever-retreating pools of water
Through the parching desert heat.
They vanished like all our illusions,
As vain and insubstantial as the Holy Lance.
Your jousting days are over, and your dreams.
Patient survivor of famine and raging thirst,
You deserved a better pasture, Veuillantil.
Take me now to my *rendezvous* with truth.
Take me to the Tower of David
And let us, two together, summon up our strength.'

The time is opportune for Providence,
Protective and benign, to shine on Raymond.
His trusted emissary brings good news
In haste; his step is light, his eyes are bright:
'From Ifthakār, the garrison commander,
To valiant Raymond, Count of Toulouse
And Lord of St Gilles, a salutation.
To you I make the offer of surrender:
The garrison and citadel are yours.

My life is yours, but for my family
I seek safe passage from Jerusalem.'

On horseback fully caparisoned, escorted,
Count Raymond makes his way towards the Tower.
Duke Godfrey's men have hastened there before him,
Failing to gain admission; they have gone,
Snatching the prized Egyptian horses.
But Raymond's prior delegation won
The right to parley, and the bridge is down.
One by one the bolts are drawn.
The fortress door creaks open for admission.
More dressed for tournament or procession,
He climbs the stone steps, in ungainly motion,
His chainmail chafing, rasping on the walls;
Breathless, he climbs, labouring in his armour,
Till at the stairhead there stands before him
Unarmed, without a bodyguard, head bowed,
Cloaked in a jellaba, supported by his sons,
The Egyptian Iftikhār, the garrison commander.
Shocked; despite apparel, each man knows
In this moment out of time and out of war
That he has never seen anyone so like himself,
And Raymond knows this man must live.
Iftikhār advances, kneels, his sword
Held flat; he lays his sword between them.
They speak no words, but innermost thoughts they share.

Descending, Raymond feels renewed, assured;
He orders Iftikhār, his family and his men
To be spared: 'Treat them with dignity;
Escort them from the Tower in safety;
But expel them from the city;
Give them safe passage;
And let Iftikhār return to the Fatimids.
Should Iftikhār rejoin the Egyptian army,

He will never be my enemy.'
And whether Iftikhār sailed to Alexandria,
Or met the advancing army on its way
To Ascalon, no one can say.

Picture a procession:
Duke Godfrey, barefoot like a pilgrim;
Tancred, under Godfrey's command
And stand-in for Bohemond;
And jealous Count Raymond,
And Robert of Normandy and Stephen,
And all their Christian warrior priests,
Servants leading the horses
Clip-clopping on the pilgrim way
That takes the warriors to the Holy Sepulchre,
Picking their way daintily among the bodies,
To thank God for their victory;
Picture their surprise
To find the Holy Sepulchre unharmed,
The edifice neglected, not despoiled
By evil infidels,
The three years longed-for shrine
Untouched by any sign
Of desecration.
If Urban and his legate Adhémar had known!
Or known how death would supervene.

Within a city ravaged and despoiled,
The streets awash with Muslim blood,
Within the aura of the longed-for Holy Sepulchre,
The Frankish princes and their priests
Assemble for a litany of prayer
And sing a new song unto their Lord,
Clapping their hands in ecstasy;
Together, in a *cantus planus*,
They sing the pilgrim-warrior hymn

Veni Creator Spiritus,
And the Office of the Resurrection,
And then a joyful Gloria
And a *Dona nobis pacem*
To celebrate the liberation of Jerusalem.
And it is no wonder, a thousand years later,
That Muslims, weary of invaders,
Call us, with curling lip, 'Crusaders'.

Cathars

I

Another age, another Pope,
Another cleft in Christendom;
Another armed crusade;
Another hive of humanity destroyed.

The Cathars rule their own church,
Appoint their own bishop,
Dispensing with the sacraments,
And do so with impunity!
How dare these half-believers,
Unregulated, unaccountable,
Brazenly independent of Rome,
Indifferent to perfection in their name,
Pollute the pure clear waters of the Holy See?
How dare they defy the Curia?
And who will expunge their heresy?

Only an expert Inquisitor from Spain,
Impeccable in his piety,
A churchman through and through,
Primed in scholastic theology,
Astute, austere and incorruptible:
None better than the saintly Dominic
Who with his fervent followers,
The feared, fanatical Black Friars,
Known among heretics as 'The Hounds of God',

Who love their work and take no pay
According to their rule,
Will detect and correct each evil heresy
And aided by the notary
Will formally deliver judgement on each heretic,
Young or old, among the Albigenses.

Let the campaign begin.
The Friars are permitted in their method
To apply a modicum of persuasion
If necessary, to extract confession.
They welcome any sign of recantation
And specify the penance due
And how it should be done, according to the book.
Here's guidance: *'Listen and take heed.*
You must answer carefully.
Answer correctly and you'll live to see another day.
This is not the time
For querying a word or text.
You cannot argue with God.
Your life in this world and the next
Depends on what you say.
But if your answer's incorrect,
You must expect the punishment you deserve,
An *auto-da-fé*
For heresy.
It's in the market-place outside.
The fire is ready to be lit.
But we grant you one concession
When making your confession:
Give us the name of someone you suspect
And you will not be burned.
First, is Jesus man or God?
And next, the world that we live in, is it evil or good?

Third, do you acknowledge and accept
The grace of God imparted through the sacraments?
And finally, will you in your life and in your heart
Obey the Holy Roman Catholic Church?'
The Hounds of God worked long and hard,
Preaching to ignorant villagers
Unconscious of their sin,
Suspicious of strangers,
And teaching curious and gullible children
How to inform against their elders.
But for all their dedicated labours,
The Friars had little to show
But a handful of tearful confessions,
And mumbled recantations
Marred by their incredibility,
Until a murder forced a furious reckoning.
Peter of Castelnau was the papal legate, and his killing
So provoked His Holiness to anger
That Innocent III called down an armed crusade;
The time was right for righteous retribution
And the reordering of this patch of Christendom.

The nobles and vassals, the knights and retainers,
The militias and mercenaries of Northern France,
Together with their clerics and servants,
The cooks and customary camp-followers,
The hangers-on and would-be pillagers,
The rabble and the scavengers,
Responded to the holy call.
They faced eight hundred miles of stony roads,
But these were worn and well-marked tracks;
For three days in the South, the sirocco blew;
And twenty thousand men came to a halt;
But this was no haphazard expedition;
It was, praise God, a Pope-appointed mission,
And its leader was his legate, Abbot Amalric.

So it transpired, that one fine summer's day,
The vanguard of this armed crusade drew up
Before the battlements of Béziers.
Two hundred Cathars sheltered there
In hope of sanctuary, and toleration,
Among the Catholic population.
A siege was imminent, and provoked defiance;
Defence was weak, the spirit strong;
As if oblivious of the danger,
The citizens wanted no negotiation
With the Northern armed invader;
That was their greatest blunder.
The stand-off was precarious and could not last:
This tree had only to be shaken
For crusaders to gather the fruit;
It was the rabble and the pillagers
Who flung themselves at the walls;
The guards and sentries fled; the gates broke upen;
The undefended town was ripe for plunder;
Armed crusaders flooded in,
Brandishing swords and ready to use them,
Eager for the spoils and rewards of war;
No mood to mark one victim from another;
High on adrenalin, compulsively driven
As predators in pursuit of the defenceless,
Rejoicing in slaughter;
And when the citizens fled in terror,
Catholics and Cathars alike,
Women weeping, babies wailing,
Seeking the shelter of their last illusion,
The untouchable refuge
Under God's protection,
The consecrated holy ground,
The sanctuary of the cathedral,
Beseeching God to save them,
The papal legate, Abbot Amalric, declared,

'Kill them all, God will know his own',
And the church became a place of execution,
And Béziers became a byword for carnage.

II

Another generation
Hounded by the Inquisition;
Another expedition
Appointed as their nemesis.

Perched on the lofty crag of Montségur
Sit crumbling turrets and collapsing walls;
For this was once both fortress and château,
Home of a dream, site of surrender.
The Cathars had smelt the smoke
Of burning at the stake
And heard the cries of torture;
Sick of a life of suspicion and fear,
Too maddened to care about the consequences,
A band of Cathars wilfully betrayed
Their own philosophy; they stalked, waylaid
And killed the leader of the Inquisition,
Thereby ensuring double penalty for sin;
For this offence in both domains,
Coupling the spiritual with the temporal,
Invited punishment at its most extreme:
Denunciation and retaliation
From God's true representative in Rome,
And retribution on earth
Without the hope of Heaven.

And it was mightily convenient for Louis IX
To assemble a force to subjugate the South
With the blessing of His Holiness the Pope;
A sovereign must assert his sovereignty;

Cities and towns must plead their loyalty;
Taxes must be levied, and lands are there for the taking;
It's time to plan another armed crusade.

The Cathars in their hive at Montségur
Had built a close community,
Sustainable, but unprepared for war:
Families with children, servants, friends,
Catharists, and the Cathar core;
They thought their misty mountain-top secure,
Inaccessible, except to mountain goats
And nimble climbers like themselves;
But then the armed crusade appeared,
Banners, pennants and crosses held aloft,
Knights in their panoply, horses caparisoned,
Lances and halberds flashing in the sun,
A gaudy cavalcade,
Ten thousand men equipped to start a siege,
Formidable!

And so began the business of blockade,
The process of attrition,
The strategy of starvation,
Enlivened by assaults and testing of defences,
Until, while on reconnaissance,
A scouting-party found a secret route
That took them to the misty top.
The Cathars, unified by faith, would not recant.
The soldiers led two hundred of the Cathar core
Down from their lair at Montségur
And penned them in a palisade of fire.
And so it came to pass that in the fulness of their heresy,
The Cathars ceased to be.
It was for the good of their souls, you may be sure,
That they were annihilated.

St Bartholomew's Day

Her daughter Marguerite was sister to the King of France,
And she herself the Regent.
Her son-in-law was Henry of Navarre,
The champion of reform.
What Catherine de Médicis hoped for
In the union of a Catholic with a Huguenot,
A worthy Protestant,
Was the promise of peace
For a divided nation:
The wedding vows, the holding hands,
Would signify the ties that bind
And serve as notice of a treaty to be signed;
And should the comely pair perform their duties as they ought,
And Marguerite have issue, God be praised,
A royal generation and a noble court
Would in the diadem-encrusted future honour her,
Queen Mother, as mentor and progenitor.
What Catherine de Médicis expected
Was a living tapestry of reconciliation,
With feasting, jesting, courtly dances,
Stately pavanes, galliards, light-stepping voltas,
Graced by her band of sweet-voiced violins,
And dresses embroidered with pearls,

With *tableaux vivants* and pastoral processions
Invaded by wanton satyrs, coy nymphs and nereids,
And dancers sprinkling the royal pair with rose-petals
In the warm air filled with the chiming
And counter-chiming of church bells.
Yet one black night
Destroyed her reputation
And rent the fabric of the nation.
For what she did, or would or could not do,
Would carelessly ignite
A leaping fire of horror
And torch another civil war.
Whether she was trapped, as in a net,
A nexus of complicity,
Of confusion or collusion,
Writhing now this way, now that,
Remains unsure, obscure.

As holder of the Regency,
Her marrow was invaded by that chill infection
Known as insecurity,
Begetter of fearful dreams:
Pursued by wolves,
Or drowning in a sea of severed heads,
Or being locked away
For ever and a day.
She must change her physician,
Acquaint herself with spies,
Protect herself with edicts and decrees,
Promulgations without precedent,
Recensions, abolitions,
And thoughtless contradictions;
What lay behind each new surprise announcement,
No one could say.
Anxiety conceived an ill-considered stratagem
To eliminate the opposition;

Her vision clouded and her values first and last
Became politicised.
But this was the palace and this was the court
Where not a word remained unheard
By those not meant to hear it.
Every whisper wafted through some window,
Down some dark passageway;
Every half-formed wish was amplified
Into an echoing misinterpretation,
Every slight remark mulled over,
Sipped and savoured over a befuddling cup
And every plot provoked a counter-plot.
The Catholic Lords conspired against the Huguenots
Who came to witness and rejoice.
Guns will be fired, but not in royal salute,
Instead, the guns resound
As signal to commence the work of retribution.
And bells will ring, but not in rejoicing,
Only to confirm that all the killing work is done.
Some few have left too soon,
And these are spared.
But each remaining wedding guest,
Each Huguenot, is killed,
To the chiming
And counter-chiming of church bells.
Intolerance and violence
Erupt like the plague,
Soon to contaminate
The whole of France,
And thousands more are slain.

'The bodies that you see there,
Floating down the Seine,
My Queen,
Those are bodies of the Huguenots.'
'My good lord, I hear and grieve;

This news has come too late;
The river in full flood
Cannot wash away the blood
Or flush the guilt away,
For this
Is Saint Bartholomew's Day.'

Drogheda

'Trust me', said the Lord Protector.
'The bloody business of a massacre
Makes victory no sweeter.
Whatever I ordered at Drogheda,
No one can call it a crime;
Like the pacification of Wexford,
Rebellion and punishment fit together;
I call it *The righteous judgement of God*;
It was right, it was just, at the time.'

17. Portrait of Oliver Cromwell (1599-1658) by
Sir Peter Lely. (It was from Samuel Cooper that Cromwell
commissioned a portrait 'with warts and all').

Glencoe

Iain of Glencoe in the Highlands,
Chief of the MacDonald clan,
Had flinched at an oath of allegiance
To become a King William's man.

Old Iain lacked friends in the Highlands,
Beset by enemies round and about;
They fed their feuds like fires in the winter
And fanned them so they would never go out.

The King lacked affection for Scotland:
It lay like a curse on his head;
He despised the whole tribe of MacDonalds:
'That set of thieves!' I wish they were dead.

The Master of Stair was his agent in Scotland,
In league with the MacDonalds' foes;
He would take any bold course of action
To bring this affair to a close.

With royal authority forcing
The last of the clans into line,
Iain went at first to Fort William,
Then missed the date when he needed to sign.

The King's Men were enlisted in Scotland,
The best of the Campbell clan;
These Campbells enlisted as soldiers,
But stayed true to the Campbell clan.

The Master of Stair gave instructions
To bring the King's men to Glencoe,
And to billet them with the MacDonalds,
But their friendship was only a show.

Iain welcomed them, still unsuspecting,
And they stayed for twelve nights and twelve days,
There was drinking and feasting and dancing,
With never a thought as to who pays.

Then one morning the soldiers rose early,
Before the lark rise in the glen,
Their orders, 'To root out the Macdonalds',
To slaughter their hosts there and then.

The sons have escaped at the first breath of treachery;
The soldiers press on with their villainous plan;
These guests, who are now executioners,
Will destroy the MacDonald clan.

They have slaughtered the women and children,
They have murdered the Chief of the clan,
Old Iain of Glencoe in the Highlands,
Turned a King William's man,
Iain of Glencoe in the Highlands,
Murdered, the Chief of the clan.

Culloden

If only the presence of the Prince
Had faded into the mist, long since,
Here on this low and open ground,
On dark Drummossie moor,
With the shouts of conflicting commands,
Amid the thump of cannon and crackle of muskets,
The wild battlecries, the pounding of hooves,
The clashing of claymores, slashing of bayonets,
The whinnying of horses and screams of the wounded;
Till with his weak and starving Highlanders
Disordered, on dark Drummossie moor,
The loser fled. For it was here that the Prince
Of his own free choice
Took from his favourite the worst advice
And set out his Order of Battle here,
On this low and open ground,
Advantage to his adversary,
Who grasped the day
And gave his grateful nation and his King
A brutal and a lasting victory.
If only, on this low and open ground,
The clansmen were not buried here;
Each clan with its own green mound,
On dark Drummossie moor.
Then, curious visitor,
Or sentimental kinsman, sometime Highlander,
The skirl and wail of the pipes might never arouse you.

The vision of Redcoats and tartans might never confuse you;
Or in your innocence
You would keep your distance
From the faint presence of the Prince.
For here, if you speak to the spirit of the rebel Highlander,
He will speak to you
Of how he fought for the Young Pretender
In this very spot where he was blasted
By the cannon of the Duke of Cumberland,
And here, where the maimed and wounded
And dying lay untended,
The Redcoats bayonetted and clubbed them,
Showing no mercy;
And from here, wherever the survivors fled,
The Redcoats hunted and hounded them
As if they were animals,
Over the dark moorland, the dykes and the bogs,
Hounded the last of the clansmen, and their kinfolk,
Into the withies and shelter of bothies,
Showing no mercy;
For William Augustus, Duke of Cumberland,
Despised the King's enemies and took no prisoners;
He quelled the rebellion with hangings,
Burnings, dispossessions and summary executions,
So that his soldiers might enjoy 'the sweets of victory'.
And for these glorious demonstrations
Of the unity of nations,
The 'Conquering Hero' of Culloden
Is not forgotten,
Nor is the tragic Prince,
Emblem and agent of his own lost cause.
And both these warriors were twenty-five years old.

'Peterloo' 1819

I

A shimmering disc, a blur in blue,
But coming into focus, gradually,
A bold familiar shape and image:
And now the plaque appears with clarity:

Official recognition with a guarantee,
A record of our heritage.
Like plaques that honour some celebrity
Or celebrate some feat of courage,

Heroism, or selfless bravery;
With just sufficient time to gauge
The brief description of a huge assembly
And its 'dispersal' by 'the military',

Inscribed in words purporting to be true:
An intervention, no doubt necessary
In case of crowd behaviour, deemed unruly,
Descending into riot and a hullabaloo;

A flash of banners activates the screen,
Winging like a flock of passing birds;
One word is caught,
The word is 'Vote…'
And then, in a *mêlée* and a rout,
There flutters down across the scene

With other revolutionary words
A banner with the title, 'PETERLOO'.

Their lordships missed the point.
So did His Royal Highness, long ago;
If law and order meant
The killing of the innocent,
Cui bono?
Though, in the marketing of entertainment,
There's tension and excitement
In the climax of this one big scene;
It's epic in its grandeur,
With cast of thousands, mingling, gossiping,
A festive crowd, in holiday mood, milling
And overspilling
From Saint Peter's Fields;
It has the makings of a motion picture
And needs the full wide screen;
The multilayered crafting, scripting,
Editing, cross-cutting,
For the film that's waiting to be made,
Calls for a master of the art of film
To compose every frame,
To insist on his personal vision
From first treatment to post-production;
Another David Lean;
With telling close-ups of the human face,
The face in the crowd, the individual,
And emphasising the visual
When the story goes political;
Intercut a single shot of sharpening a sabre, carefully;
Applause and cheers for the orator, arriving,
Climbing the steps to the hustings, waving,
With friends and supporters, peacefully,
And a pan and scan of the banners at the meeting;
No cheers for Manchester magistrates, watching,

Impatient to issue the fatal order:
'Arrest the orator!'
Cut to gallant yeomen entering their favourite hostelry,
Insolent in their blue and white uniforms,
Doffing their shakoes,
Quaffing ale with oaths and ribaldry,
Emerging with sunlight on their sabres,
And a trial swishing and slashing of their sabres,
Patting their restless horses,
Mounting their horses unsteadily;
Then track the mother and babe-in-arms,
The little boy about to die.
The calm before the violence.
A tracking shot as the cavalry break into a canter.
Slow-motion as the horses break into the crowd.
Forward to the trumped-up accusation:
Roles for bigwigs, 'just-assés', characters,
Tipsy yeomen, hired informers;
Roles for orators and charismatic speakers,
Both in public and in Parliament.
Flash back to the moment of arrest,
Underplayed by famous actors;
Forward to Orator Hunt's release, on bail,
A little pale;
An interior of Ilchester gaol;
A time-lapse of two and a half years,
Then back again for the travesty of a trial.
The narrative presents a precious gift
To writer, designer, costumier,
Photographer, and political philosopher,
A showpiece courtroom drama
With collisions of law and principle,
Rich in symbols and talking at cross-purposes,
With golden nuggets of gobbledegook
And Latin terminology
To confound and confuse the ignorant,

With diversions, delays and ponderous wit,
Deflating high hopes, inflating human fears,
On a stage ready-made for legal pomposity,
With strutting actors, officers, walk-on performers
And the King's soldiers on guard at the door,
While under the smokescreen of legal formality
The spirit of Sidmouth is tilting the scales
And a voice-over speaks with acidity:
'I hope the proceedings at Manchester
Will prove a salutary lesson
To these modern reformers'.
All this, for shooting on location,
With the budget under strain,
A temperamental star, and the usual rain.
The point lies not in the sudden slicing of sabres
Into the fragility of life:
Eleven dead, five hundred wounded,
And the absence of emergency services;
Still that is not the point.
The point lies in justice denied,
Authority misapplied,
All in the name of law and order;
Truth compromised, violence legitimised,
All in the name of law and order.
So for a thoughtful ending,
Over the rightful, blood-red second plaque,
In silence, let the credits roll.

II

The Royal George, 18th August, 1819
The Prince Regent, to his Private Secretary.
Gad, Sir!
Tell them to keep the post-chaise waiting.
That numskull Sidmouth wants a letter.
He pesters me like a dog at the heels of its master.

I knew it ! My worst possible choice of Minister.
Intolerable fellow, he shall have it.
But first, in my own hand, a more agreeable matter:
To Lady Hertford, with the Royal Seal of Hanover,
And double-sealed with a kiss. See that it goes today.
My waistcoat is splitting. I need a new tailor.
What is this dank, rebellious town called Manchester
Where they throw stones and break windows for their sport !
Like the rioters, the Nottingham frame-breakers,
Nothing but ill-bred rabble and trouble-makers.
And now Manchester. What kind of a town is this,
With neither a Duke nor a Duchess !
Not a gentleman among 'em.
Peopled by vagrants, feeding on groundless grievances,
Drunkards delighting in noisy disturbances.
Bumkins and blackguards, all of 'em !
I'd have them taken to Newgate and hanged.
These ballads and broadsheets are scurrilous,
The cartoons are scandalous, the lampoons are libellous.
Zounds and blood! Give me pigeon and beef pie for supper,
Two flagons of port, cherry brandy, and water.
Prepare me a missive.
To the Right Honourable the Lord Sidmouth.
And say that I, His Royal Highness etcetera,
Do earnestly command your Lordship
To convey to the Lords of Derby and Stamford
My warm appreciation, and high commendation,
Of the magistrates and civil authorities
Who on this most dangerous occasion
Preserved the peace in Manchester.
And when the time is come,
Their Lordships will know who I am.
I will have a coronation
The like of which the world has never seen.
And furthermore,
His Royal Highness wishes to commend

The loyal and fearless Major Trafford
Of the Manchester and Salford Yeomanry
For his personal bravery
In upholding the sanctity of the law,
Like all good citizens who defend
The safety of the realm, etcetera.
Their vigilance and circumspection
Have saved us all from insurrection.
In times of unrest we do our best.
All troublemakers should face arrest.
I'm sure that any minor injury
Was borne out of necessity
And entirely the fault of the injured party.
God save us all from harm
Disguised as radical reform.
May God preserve the *status quo*.
The love you bear your Prince
Will be rewarded, certainly.
Here's a health unto His Majesty !
Long live His Majesty, at present indisposed.
And here's another. Here's. Here's.
Meantime, aboard the Royal Yacht
At Chichester, by God! it's too d – d hot.

The Battleship Potemkin

All film is fiction.
When fiction's twice removed from truth
And more than half political,
It's propaganda.
But when a film is made with passion
It demands and receives attention.

This is a film that teaches
How it should be read:
'There are no maggots in this meat!'
The First Lieutenant said.
But he knew, and we knew
And the whole ship's company knew
That this was outrageously untrue.
For Eisenstein, it represents official lies,
But that should come as no surprise.

And when, in splendid uniforms in white,
With braided collars buttoned tight,
And bayonets fixed,
The Tsar's most loyal Cossacks, ranged in line abreast,
Descend the Odessa Steps, with orders, not to arrest
But to shoot first
And to clear the public from the public place,
We understand the cause of revolution
And receive it in the impact of the images:
The silent scream, the shattered spectacles,

The baby in the runaway pram;
Images that reverberate
Through many a lesser film.

For Eisenstein, there lay within his lexicon
Varieties of truth, varnished or unvarnished,
Not simply literal, sometimes historical,
More often metaphorical.

But that's not all:
There is a continuum of knowledge,
A high and slender bridge
Crossing the sheer ravine
Dividing fact and fiction.
Correctness says, *Potemkin* shelled Odessa first,
A fact omitted from the shooting script.
If that were all,
And if his film were only propaganda
We would decode his message,
Dismiss the subtext and the discourse,
And admire the *mise en scène*,
Passing swiftly on.

That there was a massacre, there is no doubt,
Yet not at this prime location;
The cinematic setting asks to be forgiven;
Reconstructions, re-enactments, both are out;
No one forgives the massacre.

Armenia

Be born with the wrong ethnicity
And expect the worst;
You may bring on your head
Unimaginable cost.

The Turkish Armenians were caught
And systematically expelled,
Families dispersed,
An Exodus enforced.

Policemen hurry them.
Guards harry them,
Soldiers drive them
Into the desert, a long way from home.

Heat, dust and hunger have exhausted them
Before the soldiers kill them.
White bones are all that are left of them,
In the Syrian desert, a long way from home.

Why were Armenians nowhere to be seen
In Armenia, 1915?
A dangerous question, best deflected;
A delicate topic, best avoided.

This was a template for ethnic cleansing,
A demonstration of people-disposal,

A precedent for culture-extinction,
A model of existence-reversal,
A bench-mark and a blueprint
For population disappearances.

Amritsar

At Jallianwallah Bagh,
A square in Amritsar,
Protesters gathered for a peaceful demonstration,
Knowing protest was against the law;
According to one estimation,
Ten thousand at the rally.
And, representing British rule,
The British military,
Led by a b - - - - - d of the old colonial school,
Brigadier-General Sir Reginald Dyer,
A stickler for the regulations:
Crack-of-dawn kit inspections,
Drill, drill, drill,
Correct salutes and polishing boots,
Heat-of-day marches and military exercises,
Church parades and unpleasant surprises.
It was he, to satisfy the law
And save the British Empire,
Who gave the order, 'Open fire !'
Some fell there and then,
While others rushed
And were crushed
In the stampede
To escape by the way they came in;
And others fell to the snap and crackle
Of the rifles of his men,
Just soldiers
Obeying orders,
Who kept on loading and reloading

While the Sikh women kept on screaming,
Their saffron-coloured cholas blotched and streaming
With their own blood.

'Permission to speak, Sir!
The dust is rising, our men are choking
And tiring.
When do we stop firing?'
'Look', said the Brigadier, perspiring,
His pistol smoking,
'Follow the Regulations by the book.
In future, do not speak without permission,
And keep on firing
Till you have used up all your ammunition.'

For the Sikhs, in their capital city,
Home of the Golden Temple,
Heart of their religion,
The prohibition of the rally
When we were not at war
Had breached their liberty.
The record of the tally:
Over three hundred and four score.
At home, a Commission condemned him.
Had not Sir Reginald Dyer
Ordered Indians to crawl,
To show who's born higher?
But the House of Lords applauded him
For keeping Indians in their proper station,
And the public rewarded him
And honoured him
With a generous donation
For a rightful demonstration
Of colonial subjugation,
Remembered on a plaque in Amritsar.

Nanjing (Nanking)

Who gave the order to kill
All the Chinese in Nanjing ?
'It was I,' said the Japanese Emperor,
'I, in my divine authority,
I gave the order to kill
All the Chinese in Nanjing.'

18. The commander of the Imperial Japanese Army in the massacre at Nanjing, also known as the Rape of Nanjing, was General Prince Asaka Yasuhiko (above), uncle of Emperor Hirohito by marriage, and acting in the name of the Emperor.

Oradour-sur-Glâne and Distomo

Remember the citizens of Oradour-sur-Glâne,
In western France.
By way of reprisal
For the spirit of resistance
In the country that they loved,
And for actions not of their making,
Their village was chosen at random
For a sudden visit from the merciless
Special Police,
A punitive force,
Priding itself on efficiency,
With orders to enact, with extreme prejudice,
Without a hearing and without redress,
Vengeance and unmitigated violence
On men, women and children in their helplessness.
The villagers died *en masse.*
And the invaders in their thoroughness
Razed the village to the ground,
Leaving only a few charred sticks, black stones,
And a smoking quietness.

By some malign coincidence,
In that same war,
On that same day,
At Distomo, near Delphi, in Greece,
In exercise of vengeance,

With wanton violence,
And mindless purposelessness,
A whole community
Had its light put out.
An ossuary tells the tale.
Remember all the lives extinguished then,
At Distomo in Greece
And Oradour-sur-Glâne
In France.

Hans Friedrich and Yad Vashem

I watch the screen
And hear a former soldier claim
That his mind was disengaged and numb,
Desensitised,
When victims stood in ragged lines before him,
Traumatised,
Shepherded before him,
Waiting to be shot.
Carefully, he took aim.
Nor did he feel in any way to blame
For all the killing.
Hans Friedrich is his name.
His life continues just the same.
But theirs did not.

At Yad Vashem, Jerusalem,
You may visit a museum
With a record, unimaginably vast,
Of the blackest past,
Where photographs
Once taken in the family
Or at some ceremony
As before the Passover,
Or for a boy, at his bar mitzvah,
Are with each victim's name
Assembled in mosaic order,
As if each human tessera

Would speak, expressively,
Both of its own humanity
And with a more than human eloquence,
Of the greater, darker picture.

Sharpeville

March 21, 1960:
A bitter anniversary.
In the black township
Of Sharpeville, the people keep
The cruel memory of that day.
Remember the protesters,
The protesters against the pass laws,
Remember that day,
Remember who killed the protesters;
It was the police at the police station,
The police who killed them,
Those paid to protect them;
Those who, without warning,
Turned their guns on the protesters,
It was the police who, on that bitter day,
Killed the unarmed protesters,
Whose memory the people keep alive,
In the black township
Of Sharpeville.

Marikana

And fifty-two years later,
At the Marikana mine,
The mine near Johannesburg,
When the miners made their pay claim,
And came out on strike over their pay claim,
Defying the owners,
It was the Marikana mine-owners,
Who brought in the guards, the security guards,
The private army of guards,
To guard the mines and their mine-owners;
And it was the Marikana mine-owners
Who called in the police, the casual police,
Who opened fire on the unarmed miners,
Opened fire on their fellow-citizens;
The armed and careless police,
The police who were paid to protect the citizens,
The police who were there to keep law and order;
It was the armed, casual, careless police
In their lawlessness,
Who resorted to violence,
Colluding with the mine-owners,
Serving the Marikana mine-owners
To punish the strikers
For wanting more pay,
In the massacre at the mine,
The mine near Johannesburg,
The Marikana mine.

Rwanda

And in Rwanda
It was neighbour against neighbour
When the Hutus burst in waving their machetes
And sticks and scythes,
And the Tutsis fled in their thousands,
Fled for their lives,
With nowhere to hide
Except in a church,
The holy refuge, the inviolable sanctuary
Where their God could save them;
If only their God would save them!
'Help us, Lord!'
The women cried;
'Save us, save us in our hour of need!',
The men implored;
But all were trapped inside.
And the air was cleft with their cries for mercy,
Their cries unheard,
Till their pleas were severed
By the rise and fall of machetes,
And all Rwanda fell, divided,
The prayers of the faithful, unanswered.
But this is the half-story,
As told by the Tutsis, the eventual victors;
For the masters of half-story history
Are always the rulers
Who decide on the myth that is best for the children,

The fantasy that feeds the lesson,
The song they should sing,
The re-enactment game they play,
The creed they must chant together;
For the Tutsis in this tribal tragedy
Were equally to blame.
And still today,
Where grieving survivors
Nod as they pass their unrepentant neighbours,
Their fathers' and their mothers' executioners,
They long to know why, in the time of genocide,
Their trusted churchmen stood aside.

Uganda

And in Uganda, where the Lord's Resistance Army
Took the law into their bloodstained hands,
They enlisted boy soldiers
In a campaign of terror
That cracked the precious vessel of humanity.
Some were street-boys,
Some were nothing-to-eat boys,
Some were unwanted,
Some were abducted.
And wantonly they went to work;
How trustingly they took the oath before the shaman,
He with the snakehead
And a body like a tent of straw,
And a necklace of fangs and knucklebones
And an arm like a stick with an animal claw
For a hand, that was constantly thrusting and jabbing
While he would be constantly dancing and shaking and hissing
To summon up the spirits;
And sometimes he would suddenly roar
And give the boys a drink
That made them feel dizzy and sick.
Then came the initiation
In a circle of stones and mud
With a strange incantation
While their arms and faces were painted with blood.
How willingly they shouldered the weight of their rifles,
How proudly they slung the heavy belt with the ammunition,
How boldly they paraded.

And how the boys loved
Their lean and battle-scarred leaders
With so many tales to tell
Of how they eluded capture like slippery fish
And meted out mayhem and murder
In the villages of the Congo
Beyond the law,
And looted and burned the homes of their enemies,
Leaving their enemies dead.

Now the boys would learn to move like leopards.
They would learn the art of invisible stalking.
They would become like the big cats.
How the boys longed to follow their leader's footsteps,
And imitate his ease, his indifference to danger,
And efficiency in killing,
For whatever he asked them to do,
Like men, they were willing.
And when they invaded their own villages
It was they and their brothers
Who loaded their rifles and pulled the triggers
On their own fathers and mothers.

Batang Kali

Tell me,
Who gave the order
At Batang Kali?
Was it the company commander,
Or a junior officer,
Or was it a question
Of some other intention
Befogged in transmission,
Some fatal ambiguity
At Batang Kali?
Was there any contrition,
An official apology,
An offer of compensation
From the MoD?
Not one resignation?
Must it always be the same
When everyone and no-one is to blame?
Does the muddied water of accountability
Let the fish swim free?
Tell me,
I want to know.

Does it shine in regimental history,
Batang Kali?
Does anyone dare to breathe the name
Batang Kali?
For at the regimental gathering,
The band, in busbies and bearskins,

Plays just as loudly on,
The pipes are just as shrill,
The drums beat just as loudly,
Just as proudly.
Are there regimental marching songs
To the tune of 'Goodbye, Tipperary',
That stiffen the morale, and energise
The soldiers of the loyal Scots Guards
In their training and parading
And the necessary polishing
Of their bayonets and rifles?
Say nothing to the new recruits
But concentrate on cleaning boots.
So it is best forgotten,
Batang Kali,
With the heat, the sweat,
The terrible tropical diseases,
The disgust, the leeches,
And the aching fear when searching
For invisible adversaries
Where the enemy lies lurking
In the clinging claustrophobic tangle
Of the Malaysian jungle;
Uncomfortable memories,
Inconvenient truths,
For the loyal Scots Guards;
And best suppressed,
What happened to the villagers,
The innocent plantation workers,
Their families and their homes
At Batang Kali.

Tell me,
I want to know,
For those who did not go.

'Bloody Sunday'

'Bloody Sunday' they call it, even today,
In Londonderry,
Occasioned by a civil rights parade,
A peaceful parade,
In Londonderry.
But the authorities say,
After another Inquiry,
'It would be a waste of time pursuing the soldiers'.
You might think, so many years have passed,
The soldiers hoped to hear the last
Of all the quibbles and the squabbles
That so unfortunately cast
A slur upon their conduct in the line of duty.
Civilians always fail to grasp, you see,
That nothing could be more unsoldierly
Than undermining confidence
And the spirit of *camaraderie*
And solidarity
Within a fighting force
Confronting an enemy:
Their *esprit de corps*;
Say no more;
It's the morale that matters most,
Besides the target practice,
When going into action;
Morale provides cohesion;
Even a peace parade would look provocative

In Londonderry,
And further questioning would be
Invidious and unnecessary.

Policing demonstrations, you may say,
Is not the paratroopers' *métier*.
It was most unfortunate
If any innocent civilian
On this harmless demonstration
Was mistaken for a moving target,
And came into the line of sight
Of weapons aimed in his direction,
And even more unfortunate
If anyone got shot
On this parade
While giving aid
To someone wounded;
And those who turned their backs upon the dead
While fleeing to escape arrest
Could only be the enemy,
That bloody day in Londonderry.

But after this engagement,
For the record and to their credit,
Be sure the paratroopers all returned
To barracks quite unharmed
And fighting fit,
And kept their anonymity.

Srebenica

If you call it a *march*, my friend,
Then words are misleading
And 'march' has lost its meaning.
This was a desperate life-or-death flight
Of refugees, shot at by day
And terrorised at night.
Freedom was just too far away.
Bullets did more than kill;
You cannot comprehend
The depth of our despair;
You were not there;
The bullets buried hope.
Mass graves mark out the route of our escape
Where most of us met our end.
This is a tale that must be told in full,
Without forgiveness or fear,
Without a cover-up, or amnesty,
For all its inhumanity,
A tale of double hurt and injury:
The promise of protection,
The contract of security,
The lifeline of a *safety zone*
Wrongfully withdrawn.
We clamoured and hammered at their door,
Finding it shut.
The *blue berets* became invisible,
Hiding like rabbits in a warren

For their own protection,
Our hope dissolving in a puff of smoke
Like a magician's illusion.

So much for UNPROFOR,
Compliant, capitulating,
Deferring to the Scorpions,
Who carted off civilians, hundreds of civilians,
In their swaggering unopposed advance,
In the bravado and complacency of their advance,
Carting them off into camps,
Pushing and prodding them like animals:
Oh, they were brutes, these Serbian soldiers,
Claiming, 'We're only following orders';
Our fear exploded like an incendiary
Pitched into a pool of petrol.
Thousands hid in cellars,
Thousands abandoned their homes;
Panic, like a flash flood, swept through the streets;
And that was when, sheltered and shielded by the night,
Men met at Susntari,
Still unguarded, unprotected,
And planned the great escape to Tuzla,
All seventy miles away, next day;
It was take what you can and get out or die.
Thousands abandoned the town in terror,
With what they could carry,
And without a leader,
Citizens diminished in a single hour,
Reduced to refugees, in their own country.
Ours was a flight from fear into grief.
We walked until exhausted,
And slept that night by the roadside.
Next day, intercepted,
As we might have expected,
We were an easy target

Picked off by Serbian snipers,
And when too many surrendered,
Some say there were two hundred,
They were marched into the woods,
Off the road and out of sight,
Only to be executed;
As they might have expected;
And we heard their cries and the cracking of gunshots
Ringing through the woods
As the Serbian soldiers ensured that every one,
Each one, young or old, man or boy,
Was efficiently executed.
In fear, the march moved on:
This was no march, only progress in disorder.
And we were some of those who broke away,
Plunging off-road into overgrown ditches,
Struggling through thorns and thickets,
Passing deserted farms, untended fields,
Abandoned wagons, broken fences;
Our land had become a wilderness
Where we wandered, starving,
Barely existing, gathering berries,
Grubbing for mushrooms, leaves, snails,
Digging up roots, and gulping river water,
Every day a reminder that those who save themselves
Have left their otherselves behind;
Till in the meanest months, a harsh season later,
We turned, and in the sickening winter
Retraced our sad steps,
Finding the road by which we came:
Creeping unseen as if from banishment,
Shielded and sheltered by the night,
Only to find our town depopulated,
Silent and unlit, inhabited by dogs.
But in the morning, here and there,
A window or a door would half-open

In a narrow neglected street,
And a wrinkled face, still wracked with fear,
Would cautiously appear;
And some old woman, left alone,
Forgotten, destitute and dispossessed,
Would tell a tearful story;
And make these rough and bearded vagrants
Welcome, as exiles coming home;
But most of all, lamenting, grieve
For sons and daughters relatives and friends,
In a weary roll-call of the missing:
Marika, Tanja, Magda, Bruno, Jano, Slobodan,
Lost or disappeared.
And we had a tale to tell,
Of life on the edge of humanity,
For the world must know,
And the world will know, in full.
And now, each year,
Survivors of the massacre,
We gather for the anniversary,
To hold a march, but call it what you will,
For us a kind of pilgrimage;
We start the trek at Tuzla,
All seventy miles away;
We hold a simple ceremony
By laying flowers at Potocari,
And then we head back down the trail to home,
To Srebenica.

Desiderata

For all its messiness, the latest massacre will fall
Within the confines of tradition;
Like other massacres you may recall,
It fits within a universal definition
To qualify for recognition:

It needs a programme and a cause,
A feud, a grievance or resentment,
A history of tribal wars,
The breach of an agreement,
Or hatred spiked with discontent;

It needs an issue and a provocation,
A pretext for some wilful killing,
Such as the cleansing of a nation;
An underclass; and mindless willing
Agents of blood-spilling;

As much as it needs machetes, guns or knives
It needs an abrogation of the law,
Indifference to human lives,
An ideology worth murdering for;
What is a massacre but a one-sided war?
Helpful, the thirst for revenge; the opportunity
To kill first; ask questions, never;
And a deficit of empathy;
These are Desiderata
For a massacre.

19. *The Massacre of the Innocents,* by Peter Brueghel (1566?) (p.33).

20. Satirical print, *Manchester Heroes,* by George Cruikshank (1819) (p.79).

Epilogue

Love all, trust a few,
Do wrong to none.

The Countess of Rousillon in
Act I, Scene I of Shakespeare's
All's Well That Ends Well.

Remembrance Sunday
(Based on a BBC broadcast)

The heart of London, on a still autumn morning.
The Queen will lay her wreath on behalf of the nation.
The London Eye has stopped turning.
In Horseguards Parade, with marchers assembling,
A field-gun fires a salute, a signal, a warning,
A single resounding shot, with a double-thump
As the echo claps round the cityscape
From office block to office block,
Where taxis and buses are still moving;
The echo travels down from Trafalgar Square
To Whitehall and the Cenotaph, where
The crowds have gathered, still gathering,
And where the Queen will lay her wreath
On this arrested autumn morning.
For listeners and viewers at home
The same waiting,
The charged anticipation.
The gun gave the signal and the band starts playing
An almost jaunty Rule Britannia,
With cymbals clashing and drums pounding.
Now the traffic has stopped.
No traffic in Whitehall this morning.
In the centre of the thoroughfare,
Expressionless, impersonal,
Stands the Cenotaph, white as a war-grave,

Bearing standards, isolated,
Like some modern megalith
Designed for a new Stonehenge
In the heart of London, announcing
In finality of capitals, only three carved words:
'The Glorious Dead'.
Now in The Skye Boat Song the pipes are skirling
Shrilly, with the drums monotonously beating;
The Band of the Black Watch transforms a gentle tune
Into a dead tribute, lost without its lilt,
Lost without its touching words:
'Absence makes the heart grow fonder;
Isle of Beauty, Fare thee well.'
And to this tune, and 'Oft in the stilly night',
The camera takes the viewer away,
To close-ups of the members of the family
Of one young man now lost,
Who had done what he always wanted to do,
To become a soldier;
His name was Liam Riley.
And now they mourn him, his mother and sister,
And grandmother, proud of his dedication,
Killed in Afganistan;
And his grandmother said,
'Be thankful that people do remember.'
In music now, a stately theme of greater power,
Lifting the ceremony with a noble strain,
As if to take a book of patriotic pride
And open it on some glorious illustration:
The score, of course, by Elgar;
From The Enigma Variations,
The stirring ninth, Nimrod the Hunter,
Marked *Moderato*, here a funereal *Adagio*;
No strings, but with trumpets, trombones,
Euphoniums, horns, cymbals and drums,
Commanding the mood of this royal occasion;

And then, in a mood more wistful,
O Valiant Hearts, the words unsung,
Remembered by an older generation
As a patriotic military hymn,
To mark the entry of the Chapel Choir,
The boys in brilliant red and gold,
The clergy following, in procession,
(No women, only men),
In surplices so white
Against the greatcoats everywhere
In black or grey,
They seem to shine like daylight
In a world of shadow,
And shepherded, one might say,
In his ecclesiastical authority,
Bareheaded, with his staff,
And respected dignity,
By the Bishop of London.
They take their places,
In exactly measured spaces
Before the Cenotaph;
And then a royal functionary,
The Major-General of the Household Division,
Commanding two mounted regiments of cavalry
Not on parade today,
And five of Foot Guards,
Mere tokens, you might say,
Of the vast official army network under orders,
Half visible, half-hidden,
Each division and each regiment
Assigned a duty to the sovereign,
Devoted to its own tradition
In the switchback ride of history;
And next, accustomed to that ride,
Following behind him, expressionless,
The politicians with familiar faces

Fixed as though in copies of themselves
For this one show of unanimity,
Each ready to lay his wreath;
And followed by the faces of prime ministers
From long ago, proof of forgotten histories;
And close behind, the dignitaries:
Chiefs of the General Staff
And Defence Staff, rarely seen,
Encumbered with their ceremonial swords;
And the Commonwealth High Commissioners,
Surprising everyone who had forgotten
And should never have forgotten
The lands overseas, and former territories;
And then the leaders of religious denominations,
Surprising anyone mistaken
As to the changing land we live in,
Its welcoming diversity,
The colour and the richness of its flowering.
And suddenly the crowd, the dignitaries
And all participants are brought to order
With a loudly given sharp reminder,
That this is still a military occasion:
'Parade, 'Shun !'
The Guardsmen and Bandsmen are called to attention
As the ceremony lifts to another plane:
A silence, as the camera scans
The closely packed and tightlipped crowd,
Attentive, and awaiting
The entry of Her Majesty the Queen,
To lay her wreath, on behalf of the nation.
The Queen descends, in company with a King:
The King of the Netherlands has come to lay a wreath,
In tribute for his country's wartime liberation,
For this was yet another history forgotten.
And members of the Royal Family
Descend, and move to find their place assigned,

And all, except the Queen, salute the Cenotaph.
But the Queen must wait,
The Duke of Edinburgh must wait,
The Royal party must wait,
The nation must wait
For the moment when,
After the usual quarter-chimes of Big Ben
(Another momentary tension),
The first deep and resonant stroke of eleven
Synchronises with the signal of the gun
And another double clap, that echoes
From tower to tall tower
In the heart of London
For the start of the two-minute silence.
A silence for mourning or memories,
Free association, perhaps, or reflection.
I think of those Normandy cemeteries,
Where war-graves line up as if on parade,
Dressed by the left,
Headstones in uniformed hospital whiteness,
Their equalised and measured distances
Assembling a spectral regiment,
A phalanx as wide and long as the horizon,
Frozen in time,
Where relatives, hushed, searching,
In twos and threes, breathing,
Repeating, seeking a family name
Will eventually find their reminder
Of a loved one,
Identified, but lost in a numbness,
His lived identity distant,
His presence removed,
Or they must scan an endless alphabet
Of strange, dissociated names
Carved on plaques bigger than houses
For the one inscription

That justifies their journey,
Where even the lettering is dressed in uniform,
Summoned to parade, and drilled to obedience,
Difficult to take home, impossible to embrace;
These are acts of remembrance
In conception and intention;
Like outward acts, in the public domain,
Attending and marching in the veterans' parade
Where each bears witness to his own campaign
And each bears medals or some honourable ribbon,
Official reminder of a devastating war
Served in, shared in, and never to be forgotten;
A segment of a life compressed into a little token,
The trauma, tribulation and loss well hidden,
Self-censored perhaps, or beyond explanation,
Marching in groups to make their silent salute
And living tribute
Before the block of Portland stone,
The empty tomb,
To hear once again the Last Post,
On Remembrance Day, for the fallen
Whom they knew and who will never come again.
The camera takes in berets, badges, medals;
The soldiers stand to attention with fixed bayonets;
Her Majesty the Queen stands still, expressionless;
Another echoing thump from the field-gun;
And the buglers sound the Last Post, as a slight breeze
Ripples over the standards and surplices;
The soldiers rigid as statues, even spectators motionless;
Now the Queen lays her wreath, on behalf of the nation,
And some who have come for the ceremonial may feel
That this is the heart of the action.
The King of the Netherlands lays his wreath
For his country's liberation
In the Second World War.
But it is not yet time to go.

One by one, members of the Royal Family lay their wreaths.
'Parade, stand at ease! Stand easy.'
One by one, the politicians lay their wreaths.
And the Secretary of State for Foreign Affairs
Lays the only wreath of flowers,
Composed of flowers from each of fourteen
Overseas Territories.
And the High Commissioners lay their own wreaths.
While here, for the viewers at home,
Distant, and ever more distant year by year
From the Second World War,
The voice-over, in a roll-call of nations,
Remembers the thousands upon thousands
From overseas who went to war,
And some from the smallest of islands,
But never returned.
And then the other service chiefs
And civilian chiefs lay their wreaths.
At this, the service begins;
Holding his staff, standing at a lectern,
Reading strongly and with dignity,
The Bishop of London takes the motley congregation
Through a short Anglican service;
For Church of England Christianity,
Allied to the monarchy,
In a land of diversity,
Remains the official religion.
The grand old hymn, 'O God our help in ages past',
Is played, and sung by those who know the words,
The crowd half-responding. A drum-roll:
The Bishop reads the prayer of St Ignatius Loyola.
And for the vast assembly, gives a cue:
The Lord's Prayer.
But this is awkward in the open air.
And now the culmination of the ceremony:
The bugles sound a fanfare;

The massed bands play the National Anthem.
The Queen, who has laid her wreath on behalf of the nation,
And has remained standing
Throughout the silence and the service,
And has once again sustained her role impeccably,
Is free to turn and lead the Royal Family
Away from Whitehall;
The march-past may begin.
The moving image and the soundtrack say it all:
The music that the bands traditionally play,
Tipperary and the Solemn Melody,
Reveille on the bugles, and The Trumpet Voluntary;
The voice-over, annotating in a commentary
All ten and a half-thousand who,
Parading on this autumn day,
Traverse the Cenotaph and march before the nation.
The President of the Forces' Charity,
The Royal British Legion, lays the Legion's wreath,
For it is they who set the order of procession,
Regiment upon regiment:
This regimental group, that veterans' association;
To name a few: The Royal Engineers Disposal (Bombs);
The Royal Air Force; Queen Alexandra's Nursing Corps;
The King's Hussars, who crushed the rebels at Culloden;
The National Far East Prisoners of War,
And many more. The mood, for the most part, grim,
Tight-lipped, unsoftened by the crowd's applause.
For most, a show of trust in force of arms.
No lovely war for them. No flag-waving.
What they gave and had to give, more personal,
A tribute to their comrades lost or missing.
Some did not salute.
No admiration for the apparatus of authority.
Some came in wheelchairs. Some had one arm swinging.
And when the Bishop in a ringing voice
Called them in the order of the service

'To fight and not to heed the wounds',
Impossible to read the veterans' thoughts;
Some other time, some other place perhaps,
To cry out, 'Patriotism is not enough';
For there are always some for whom the raw reality of war,
As when the sea crashes on a lofty cliff,
Erodes their religion from beneath.
But then, when the last of the veterans have passed,
And the soldiers have been dismissed,
And the crowd has dispersed,
For just an hour, there hangs about the presence
Of the silent unattended Cenotaph
An evanescent sense
As fine as a sea-mist, of tragedy
Intensified by loyalty;
Would that another war could be prevented
By the laying of a hundred wreaths
And holding of a million silences.

The Field of Poppies
at the Tower of London

This field of poppies is an artist's installation.
The word has spread; few could have guessed
How ordinary folk would understand its meaning,
Out of time and out of war,
Returning home to tell their friends, 'I saw
The field of poppies at the Tower of London;
So many, like a dense and blood-red sea;
Each poppy for a soldier fallen;
I shall remember, I was there,
One of the four million
In a silence to remember, at the Tower of London.'

The Unknown Civilian

Now is also the time to remember
All those who found no shelter in the firestorm,
And all the civilians blasted to pieces
For the sake of the battleplan,
Or who fled the advancing ruin of the armoured column;
They need no monumental portico with colonnades;
No larger than life-size statues on a plinth;
They need no parades, only an unheroic monument
Of sculpted, homely figures without medals,
In any open space or parkland
Or in a station concourse,
Or in a well-loved public garden:
One, the Unknown Civilian,
Convenient target
And greatest victim of the Total War;
One, the Unknown Prisoner
Who, when arrested, simply disappeared;
One, the Orphaned Child,
The lonely, disregarded victim of the slaughter;
And in their company,
One who, driven from his home,
Forever short of food and shelter,
Shall in the devastating course
Of every conflict that resorts to military force
And every warlike operation, represent
The Unknown Refugee.

The Empty Plinth

How many lifetimes would I need
Merely to read aloud
Only the names of those who died
At the hands of the predators,
The unaccountable rulers,
The great dictators.
Only to make a start,
I would set up my soapbox at Hyde Park Corner,
Keeping apocalyptic preachers company,
Or occupy the empty plinth in Trafalgar Square
With a friend, a lunch-box and a glass of water,
And read aloud to those who might listen
And those who care,
From a text that would solely consist
Of a verified list
Of innocent lives lost
In the entrenchment of every autocrat
Who in his lust for power
And the creeping poison of his paranoia
Tramples on justice,
Makes torture a tool of government,
Imprisonment his answer to his critics
And execution his advocate.
And as each page of the list would fall

To be floated away by the wind,
My friend, who surfs the internet,
Would step up to supply me
With a new list to dismay and terrify me,
A list in forty languages and more,
A list to extend
And exceed all other lists that went before.
And he and I, alternately,
Reading in relays, would take breath;
Speak up, read on;
As if by calling out a name we might restore
The breath of life; or at the least,
A stranger in the milling crowd
Might, after half a day, exclaim,
'I knew him ! ' or 'I remember her!'
And justify the roll-call,
And suddenly give sense and resonance
To names on pages blowin' in the wind.

21. 'Teardrop', centrepiece of the Holocaust Memorial, Abbey Gardens, Bury St Edmunds – venue for the annual Memorial Day service on January 27 for all victims of genocide. It also commemorates the massacre of 57 local Jewish residents in 1190. (Opened 2015).

22. Yad Vashem, Holocaust Memorial, Mount Herzl, Jerusalem, opened 1953.

23. Hiroshima Memorial Cenotaph, Peace Memorial Park, Japan, opened 2014.

Notes and Acknowledgements

Notes and Acknowledgements

Part I: In the wild

The writer acknowledges an immense debt to the long series of Natural History programmes broadcast by the BBC on television, and one of television's greatest achievements. Besides expanding our knowledge, the series has increased our respect for the natural world and our understanding of our place in it. For Part I of *Predators: Reflections on a Theme*, the influence of the narrator Sir David Attenborough is gratefully acknowledged, as is the work of the dedicated film teams who have provided most of these images translated into words.

Beginning in autumn 2015, the seven-part TV series entitled *The Hunt* was the result of a collaboration between David Attenborough and Alastair Fothergill, dealing specifically with predators pursuing and (not always) catching their prey. To quote Fothergill in the *Radio Times*, 31 October 2015, 'There is no doubt that the most exciting behaviour in the natural world is predation. But interestingly, if you look back at films about predators, they're all the same. The predators are always red in tooth and claw, they're always the villains of the piece. What people don't ever say but which is the case is that predators usually fail. Predators are the hardest-working animals in nature. We're trying to put people into their shoes to really make them feel the challenge'. In Part 4 of the series, *Hunger at Sea*, whales, sharks, and dolphins are shown hunting; in Part 5, *Nowhere to Hide*, cheetahs and lions; in Part 6, *Race against Time*, bears are shown catching salmon, and killer whales snatching sealion pups (all relevant to *Predators: Reflections on a Theme*). Now available on DVD and as a richly illustrated BBC Book.

Taken on its own, the sequence of predatory images in Part 1 of *Predators: Reflections on a Theme* all images of hunting and killing, represents nature at its most violent. This is 'nature red in tooth and claw', in Tennyson's apophthegm from *In Memoriam* (1850), written a few years before Darwin's *On the Origin of Species by Natural Selection*. The definitive phrase that Darwin adopted to replace his own expression 'struggle for existence' was 'The Survival of the Fittest'. It was a view of nature that provided, along with a muddle of ideas originating in German philosophical idealism, a pretext for Nazi ideology and the doctrine of the Aryan 'master race'.

Part 1 of *Predators: Reflections on a Theme* looks back to that view. Fortunately, it is only part of the picture of nature available today, created by science mediated by TV, film and information technology, but it is meant to serve as a prologue to the selective vignettes and examples of human behaviour in Parts 2 and 3.

The modern reader is more equipped to see nature in the round, in all its diversity, and in its leaning towards life in balance with the environment, a life labelled by science as an ecosystem, until upset by human activity or natural catastrophe. The modern reader is less likely to politicise nature.

But to have lived in Nazi Germany in the late 1930s and 40s was to have been taught to see oneself as a member of the 'master race', involving shutting off human feeling towards whole groups of inferior fellow human beings, by reason of their nationality, birth, religion, class or political persuasion. Commentators today remain divided on an explanation why ordinary Germans under Nazi domination took so readily, and in some cases enthusiastically, to committing crimes against humanity, including war crimes on a vast scale. One thing is clear: it was less difficult for Nazi ideology to eliminate empathy than anyone might have expected.

There is no simple analogy between animal behaviour and human behaviour. There are complexities in human society such as nationalism, the pursuit of political and economic power, cultural diffferences, and the availability of fellow human beings ready to be exploited for profit or pleasure. The reader may find links both stated and unstated between Parts I, II and III.

Many of the images in *Predators: Reflections on a Theme*, Part I, are derived from sequences in *The Blue Planet* series, broadcast originally in 2001, reappearing on Yesterday TV on 2 January 2015, on BBC1 with repeats on BBC2 in 2015, on Yesterday on 3, 30 and 31 January and 6 and 7 February, 2016. *Open Oceans* features the revolving bait-balls of mackerel and sardines being herded, then attacked from below by dolphins and sharks, while simultaneously being attacked from above by diving gannets. *Blue Planet* also features the lives of turtles and squid. True, images on film can reproduce colour and movement, and film editing can supply realistic watery sound-effects, with added musical soundtrack by James Fenton on a symphonic scale, but verbal imagery, as in Predators: Reflections on a Theme, has its own if limited resources and may be able to reach below the surface. Viewers on their sofas, choosing *Frozen Planet*, will have watched ORCA, the killer whale, venturing in-shore to snatch baby seals, or working in teams to make waves to wash a seal from an ice floe. Or on another evening they could choose to watch crocodiles lying in wait to snatch animals, whether wildebeeste or zebra, on migration; to see lions overpowering an elephant; or to observe through a telescopic lens a cheetah stalking, pursuing and seizing a gazelle - all these images were captured by dedicated cameramen after hours, days or even weeks of waiting. But reflective imagery in words, as here, has more to do with chasing a unifying theme than being stunned by the spell-binding televisual action that the viewer may access using a remote control. A special note on sharks as predators: formerly viewed from a human standpoint only as a fearsome menace, typified by Steven Spielberg in his gripping and industry-changing film *Jaws* (1975), sharks are now granted respect for their intelligence and some species are shown to exhibit social behaviour, while at the same time constituting a main food source in Asia and being killed in their millions in the Far East just for their fins. Who, on this planet, are the predators?

A revised judgement on sharks is already at work in David Attenborough's *The Living Planet* (Collins/BBC, 1984), a book conceived simultaneously with the author's TV series of the same name; see the chapter on The Open Ocean, p.273. The same more objective view was persuasively presented in the BBC/ National Geographic *Wildlife Special Great White Shark* (1995), again narrated by David Attenborough. *Open Oceans* (2001) placed sharks among other predators capable of navigating great distances to their regular feeding-grounds (repeat broadcast in 2015). The controversial TV chef Gordon Ramsay should be credited for his field research in the Far East in 2011, exposing the lucrative trade in shark fins, prized strangely as a gastronomic delicacy in shark fin soup. A new series of three documentaries entitled *Shark*, broadcast on BBC and repeated on BBC 2 in 2015, was based on scientific study that revealed how some species of shark are facing extinction, including some still unidentified. A documentary on Japanese research, narrated by David Attenborough, entitled *Legends of the Deep: Deep Sea Sharks,* was broadcast on BBC4 with repeats in July 2015 and January 2016, showing living examples of previously unknown species that have survived unseen for millions of years. On Channel 5, *Deep-Sea Super Predators* showed that some killer whales predate on sharks. Evidence from Australia and South Africa suggests that danger from shark attack can be reduced by greater knowledge of shark behaviour at certain times of day and local knowledge of where they congregate for feeding. in Australia the shark is now a protected species. The Discovery TV Channel promotes an annual 'Shark Week' and between 2-7 August, 2015, this channel presented three hours of documentary films daily, culminating on 8 August 2015 in a 12-hour all-day sharkfest, while National Geographic's *Wild*, on Sky TV, presented a similar range of material. On 25 March 2016, ITV gave viewers a close-up of Britain's sharks.

David Attenborough's *Life on Earth* series began in 1979 and was likewise published in book form. His first series, a BBC co-production with National Geographic, was released on VHS tapes including, separately, *The Great White Shark, Crocodile, Eagle, Humpback Whale, Leopard, Polar Bear,Wolf* and *Tiger*. Since then the range has expanded into what are now broad categories and themes available on DVD in sets of three or four discs each, and a selection deserves to be listed here: besides the *The Blue Planet* series available in Netflix, Amazon Prime and iTunes, viewers will find *Frozen Planet, Oceans, The Life of Mammals*, including insect hunters and plant predators, *The Life of Birds*, including avian kidnappers and cannibals, *Great Wildlfe Moments*, including crocodiles and zebras, *Life Story*, including elephants and lions, or for those ready to make a major purchase, there is *The Life Collection* on 24 DVDs. A separate programme in the BBC Natural History series, *Alaska: Earth's Frozen Kingdom* shown on BBC2 TV on 11 February 2015, included the scene with grizzly bears waiting to catch salmon (an estimated 300 million) swimming up-river in the summer to spawn. The bears, we are told, gorge themselves on 40kg per day. Another separate programme, *Super-Powered Owls: Natural World*, produced and directed by Lucy Smith, shown on BBC 2 on 3 March 2015, studied 'nature's ruthlessly efficient airborne killing machines' in action and a scientific study revealed that owls possess the rare skill of silent flight in pursuit of their prey. An owl's face was compared amusingly and in some ways appropriately to a satellite dish.

A similar acknowledgement must be made to the National Geographic channels for a programme with similar content to that of the *Life on Earth* series: this was *Great Migrations: Born to Move*, from a series produced by David Hamlin and narrated by Stephen Fry, made in 2010 and broadcast on Channel 4 on 28 August 2011.

With this wealth of material to draw upon, the sequence of images of hunting in *Predators: Reflections on a Theme*, Part I, represents just one aspect of the natural world at the expense of others. For example, the astonishing behaviours of birds of paradise while courting are recorded in the first of two documentaries *Nature's Greatest Dancers*, from BBC Natural History and broadcast on BBC 1 on 26 June 2015. For courtship rituals, mating, giving birth and nurturing the young, or the rich variety of life in locations such as Madagascar, the viewer may find all these in David Attenborough's *Life* series and elsewhere. And when shooting films, cameramen set out to capture action, because editors love to use it: action at its most dramatic takes place when predators go hunting, so hunting is inevitably over-represented. Though lions spend most of their time sleeping, this is not what the viewer expects to spend leisure time watching at home on the TV screen. But such images could be used as screen savers.

Footnote: The species referred to are named for their generic behaviour. Among dragonflies, the illustration of the blue dasher is chosen to show the wing structure. For sea-turtles or green turtles, see Part 2 of the three-part series *The Great Barrier Reef*, written and presented by David Attenborough, shown on BBC 1 on 6 January 2016. To appreciate the full horror of the avian hunter-killers, refer to Ted Hughes' poem *Thrushes*, in which he also encounters a shark (*Collected Poems*, Faber and Faber, 1973, and in pamphlet No.5 of *Great Poets of the 20th Century*, introduced by Jeanette Winterson and produced by *The Guardian*, 2008).

Part II: In cities and towns

'Predators' is used in the literal sense in Part I and in a metaphorical sense in Part II. It is a metaphor that has gained a foothold for everyday purposes. As applied to human behaviour it is acquiring its own special meaning and as far as applicability is concerned, this is left to the reader to judge.

Some of the human predators in this sequence are known to have deliberately sought notoriety. A craving for power is endemic. Some have continued to exercise power by manipulating others, or by manipulating the image they have created for themselves even from inside prison.

Because, like sex, crime sells, intense media coverage has led to the rise of the celebrity criminal. A few of these human predators have become almost household names, their notoriety nursed by the media. So as to deny criminals the satisfaction of achieving celebrity status, and to focus instead on the consequences of their actions and their victims, in the verse sequence the names of individuals are omitted. There is now a distinction between those who may and those who may not be identified as a matter of public interest, following a decision of the European Court in 2013, now known as the 'right to be forgotten' (RTBF). Since that decision, the names of some living persons formerly available on the internet have been deleted. News editors, whether for the press or TV, have had to make up their minds on what is public interest (ambiguous), and have clearly come to the conclusion that serial killers and abductors, whether dead or alive, may continue to be identified. For example, Hindley (deceased) was identified by name and photograph in the *Radio Times* in October 2015, and Sutcliffe (living) in The Sun newspaper in February 2015, on TV Channel 5 in March 2015, and on 5 Star in March 2016. In these Notes, the current practice of news editors has been followed and the relevant publications have been cited in evidence.

For most members of the public, the media are the only sources of information about crime. The media create the first image of a criminal and influence the impact that any crime may subsequently have on society. The media have even in three recent instances insinuated guilt where there was none.

A 'deficit of empathy' is not an original expression and has been appropriated from the flood of popular criminology cited below. 'Empathy' is a term now in widespread use and has the great advantage of being relevant to everyday experience, in contrast to its opposites, 'sociopathy' and 'psychopathy'. These terms are sometimes used outside criminology for their quasi-scientific aura; they are not as precise as they seem and keep their subjects at a safe and uncomprehending distance. For an attempt to understand lack of empathy, and human cruelty, see *Zero Degrees of Empathy* (Penguin, 2012), by Simon Baron-Cohen. On 10 February 2015, David Wilson, Professor of Criminology at Birmingham Unversity, began a new series under the title *Psychopaths* on Channel 5 TV. (The first in the series was an exception, in focusing on a female, when over 90% of psychopaths are male). Public interest in psychopaths is both taken for granted and stimulated.

A resumé by Dr Michael Mosley of the content of earlier BBC TV programmes in the Horizon series, with the title *The Mystery of Murder: a Horizon Guide*, broadcast on BBC 4 on 9 March 2015, revealed some progress in understanding how the mind of the psychopath works, especially through the study of brain scans. But in answer to the most pressing question of all, Dr Mosley concluded that 'For the time being it seems that we cannot treat the psychopath's underlying lack of empathy'.

A new three-part series broadcast on Channel 5 under the provocative title *Meet the Psychopaths* began on 8 December 2015. It was based on Hervey M.Cleckley's seminal work *The Mask of Sanity* (1941), using video, live interviews and a 20-point grading system. It was shown to apply to a notorious businessman as well as to criminals and wartime enemies.

Page 17: Thirteen women
The media played a large part in creating fear of the so-called Yorkshire Ripper but no part in bringing him to justice. Sensational reporting was the norm. Sutcliffe was arrested in 1981 and at the trial was given 20 life sentences. Follow-up on TV has included explanations why on nine occasions he had eluded arrest. A psychological study entitled *The Yorkshire Ripper: Born to Kill?*, directed and produced by Greg Goff, has been broadcast on TV Channel 5 with repeats on 15, 25 and 27 March 2015, and on 5 Star on 20 and 26 March 2016, as though public interest, after 35 years, can never be satisfied. The matter-of-factness with which Sutcliffe referred to his crimes has been highlighted.

Also obvious is a disconnect between acts and consequences. Popular criminology relating to Sutcliffe has flourished: witness Gordon Burn's Somebody's Husband, Somebody's Son (1984); a programme on Sky 3 on 1 May 2010 in which survivors told their stories; the Channel 5 investigation shown on 28 March 2013; The Yorkshire Ripper: Crimes that Shook the World, a repeat; and a programme on the Quest Channel on 10 August 2013. As though to confirm the hold that an image can have on public opinion, on 10 February 2015 The Sun hit the news-stands with the front-page headline: 'The Grim Reaper: Sutcliffe plans his own funeral'. And media interest continued with Left for dead by the Yorkshire Ripper, featuring interviews with survivors, on Channel 5 Star TV on 5 July 2015 and repeated on Channel 5 on 24 March 2016 (see above for 26 March). BBC News 24 on 1 December 2015 had reported on his move from Broadmoor.

The murder of women by men (far more often than vice versa) is now the subject of a 'Femicide Census' (not a Home Office study), a timely systematic record of data organised by Karen Ingala Smith. The data are only part of the much larger record of acts of violence, mainly of domestic violence assaults, by men against women. The columnist Eva Wiseman writing in *The Observer* on 22 May 2015 quoted Ingala Smith as saying: 'When men kill women they are doing so in the context of a society in which men's violence against women is entrenched and systemic.' Eva Wiseman noted that between 2002 and 2012, 93.9% of adults who were convicted of murder were men. The End Violence Against Women coalition reported in *The Observer* on 29 November 2015 that services for survivors of abuse were struggling to remain open. Note: The National Association for People Abused is based in Cheltenham. Refuge, the national charity, has a website.

Page 17: One boy. Fourteen men

Nilsen killed a boy and 14 men in London in the 1970s. They were all outsiders, 'unconnected people', who would not be missed. His life and crimes were analysed in a Channel 5 TV programme on 21 March 2011 and in a 5 Star TV programme on 27 March 2015, with re-enactments.

Page 18: And there lived a couple in Gloucester

The Wests and their 'House of Horror' at 25 Cromwell Street captured the front pages of the tabloid press in 1994 and have provided material for dramatic reconstructions and investigations ever since. They have been studied in detail both as individuals and as a couple. 'Malignant and two of a kind' is a phrase borrowed from a programme made for TV by the crime writer Martina Cole, who has paid special attention in her series *Lady Killers* to Rose West 'who is currently serving a life sentence without parole for ten separate counts of murder, committed during the 1970s and 80s', posing the question, 'Could Rose have become a serial killer through circumstance, or was she just born that way?' This programme included interviews with a survivor and a criminal psychologist, and featured impressionistic reconstructions, but without any graphic detail. The programme was shown on the Yesterday TV Channel on 5 April, 2014, and was a repeat, and was given another repeat on the Alibi Channel on 31 May 2015. Addicted viewers could switch channels the same evening to watch Channel 5 Star's *When Fred met Rose*, missing only ten minutes because of the overlap (repeated on 1 November). Channel 5 had broadcast a programme on the Wests on 26 July 2012.

A series of three programmes on the pair was broadcast on Channel 5 in November 2014, the second of which bore the subtitle 'House of Horrors'. In January 1995 the front page of the *Daily Mail* had carried a familiar picture of the Wests alongside the headline: House of Horrors Man Kills Himself. On 3 August 2011, ITV broadcast an absorbing dramatisation by Neil McKay of police interviews that had taken place with West after his arrest, under the title Appropriate Adult, referring to the volunteer social worker who had agreed to be present but found herself coming under his influence. It was repeated on 23 May 2015. The *Radio Times* promotion reminded readers that this drama was made by the same team that had made See No Evil, about the Moors Murders, and This is Personal, about the Yorkshire Ripper.

Public interest seems insatiable; on Sunday 15 November 2015, Channel 5 Star offered a double bill, *The Unseen Fred West Confessions* (extracted from police interviews), followed by Fred and *Rose: the Last Betrayal*, a reshaping of existing material. The so-called confessions were repeated on 3 April 2016. On 27 March 2016, Easter Day, Pick channel offered *Fred and Rose: the Unanswered Questions*, suggesting links to earlier murders.

Page 19: And in the Market Street in Hyde

On 2 October 2011 *The Observer* carried a lengthy extract from What is Madness? by Darian Leader (Hamish Hamilton, 2011), in which the author studies the mental make-up of Shipman, who had eluded any conventional stereotype of mental abnormality. It was Shipman's ordinariness that is so disturbing. An Inquiry into the murders for which he was convicted revealed no apparent motive except that he regarded himself as the victim. Subsequent correspondence highlighted Shipman's 'stunning lack of empathy and total emotional detachment.'

A programme for Channel 5 in the Born to Kill? series on 3 July 2013 showed psychologists still looking for clues. Dr D.A.Holmes, a criminologist, summed up his theory that Shipman was a criminal who saw himself as 'Doctor God'. After Shipman had served four years in prison, still playing the doctor, he committed suicide. The tenth anniversary of his suicide was marked on 17 May 2015 by a double bill on Channel 5 Star: *Harold Shipman: Driven to Kill* and *Harold Shipman: Catching Dr Death*. The latter was repeated at 2 am on November 7/8 2015, on the TV channel entitled without intended irony, True Entertainment, also on Channel 5 Star, 20 December 2015.

Page 19: Two predatory clerks in Manchester

Here is another tragic story of serial killing that the media cannot leave alone, and not just because the victims were children. The search for bodies of the victims of Brady and Hindley kept the tabloid press busy for months, with reminders that one victim is unaccounted for even today. Their roles were mutually supportive in procuring victims, from 1963 onwards, and remain of interest to viewers and readers of what bookshops and libraries label as 'True Crime'. The fact that Brady was a Hitler fanatic provided an even more bizarre twist. The former editor of *The Observer* newspaper, David Astor, visited Hindley in prison and became a regular correspondent with her. He died in 2001 and she died in 2002, closing a strange postscript to the story of the link between the press and this grim case. In *The Observer* on 28 February 2016 his son Richard pointed out that Hindley's 25-year sentence had expired and that she was being kept in prison indefinitely by popular demand, a form of wrongful imprisonment.

Brady meanwhile remained in Broadmoor. A programme showing how Brady was still manipulating everybody, including the relatives of his victims, was broadcast on Channel 4 on 28 August, 2012. Public interest continued: on 11 July 2013, two TV programmes on the Moors murderers, a documentary under the title *Brady and Hindley: Possession*, and a drama about the same events, were broadcast on the same evening.

The first part of a three-part semi-documentary series *Myra Hindley, the Untold Story*, was broadcast in June 2015 on Channel 5, and repeated in July. It was based on Hindley's admittedly unreliable unpublished autobiography. The mix of narration with fictionalised dialogue and unconvincing action was difficult to accept other than as a presentation of crime as entertainment. Viewers could watch a repeat of part 2 of *The Untold Story* on Channel Five Star on 21 June 2015, followed next night on ITV3 by a repeat of part 1 of the two-part drama *See No Evil: The Moors Murders*, this time from the angle of the police investigation.

On 10 March 2016, Channel 5 broadcast a programme with a wider remit and one that went some way towards refocusing attention onto the victims and their families, though it did not go as far as the London Road play, musical and film have done for a community marked by crime. (See the reference to *London Road* below, under Now call to mind...). Entitled *The Moors Murders: Britain's Worst Crimes*, it began by acknowledging the interest of the public and added, 'No other crimes have left such an indelible mark on society'. But it avoided sensationalism and concentrated on interviews with the families of victims, ending with a dedication to their memory. It was written and produced by Helen Tonge.

There is yet another aspect to this case: when an identification photograph of Hindley was made public, the image was adopted by the media as a symbol of evil, 'the most hated woman in living memory', according to *The Untold Story*. From this image the modern artist Marcus Harvey created a ten times larger than life-size portrait that dominated the gallery where it was exhibited. Though almost immediately vandalised by a few members of the public, this unconventional portrait was commended by an art critic.

Page 20: Hail a taxi, name a destination

Warboys was convicted in 2009 of drugging and sexually assaulting 12 victims, though he was believed to have attacked about 100 women. Following his conviction, two of his victims claimed compensation from the police, claiming that the police investigation was flawed.

Page 20: Did you hear of the minicab driver

From one point of view, driving minicabs was only Grant's day job. His case became national news on 23 March, 2011, after he received 29 verdicts of guilty, and the Metropolitan Police apologised for not having caught him ten years earlier. It was said that he may have committed about 600 attacks. If this statistic sounds less extraordinary than it should, the reason may lie in conventional expectations about male behaviour, expectations that have remained unchallenged for as long as inequality has persisted in human society. Now in its third year, an international campaign entitled '1 Billion Rising' aims to confront sexual violence against women, mainly through dialogue and education. That there are economic, political and in some cases religious beliefs to be taken into account will surprise no one.

Page 20: The schoolgirl's unforgettable face

Burials and exhumations add to the appalling story of McLoughlin, alias Tobin. In an interview, one of his three ex-wives said that she had thought him 'charming'. When arrested by Strathclyde police for the murder of a Polish student, whose body he had dumped under the floor in a Glasgow church, he admitted that the Metropolitan and Kent police were also looking for him. Tobin is said to have once boasted of having killed 48 women. He was already in prison when on 20 December 2009 that unforgettable picture from 1991 returned to the TV screen. Channel 5's *The Untold Story*, on 19 June 2012 and 13 July 2013, covered an investigation of Tobin's record by David Wilson, Professor of Criminology, Birmingham University.

Page 21: Released for just one hour

Having previously stabbed three other people, the offender, a paranoid schizophrenic and known to be violent, had been released from a secure unit in a mental hospital, and had absconded. Police had no power to detain him because he had not been sectioned and was a voluntary patient. A photograph with details appeared in *The Guardian*, 23 July 2008.

Page 22: And another prisoner on release

The media have kept this distressing story in the public domain by interviewing the daughter who survived the attack.

Page 22: Early release for one obsessive prisoner

The case became controversial when it appeared that the offender may have been released as part of a Government programme to relieve pressure on jail places.

Page 22: Or you may have heard of the prisoner

The offender's 8-year-old stepdaughter had dialled 999 to call the police. On 5 February 2010, BBC News 24 reported that he had been jailed for life.

It has taken women to correlate the data on male violence against women and the preponderance of male murders of female victims. A full-page report on this initiative appeared in *The Observer* for 8 February 2015, noting the increasing demands on the charity Women's Aid. On 14 March 2016, BBC 1 broadcast

Behind Closed Doors, revealing the problems that police officers in Thames Valley domestic abuse units face in getting convictions in the courts, even where there is clear evidence of harm.

Page 22: And there are predators more subtle yet
This was only one of a series of tragic instances showing how much work remains to be done to alert the public, especially young people, to the dangers of internet predators who stalk victims on social networking sites: Criminal Minds, Series 5, 9 July 2010. Further tragedies made the headlines in 2015.

Page 22: In the Midlands you may have heard
The case of this offender has been echoed in results of the Savile investigation (Operation Yewtree) and in other cases of historic abuse, with victims whose reports of abuse had previously been disbelieved or deliberately covered up, only now being listened to in court. The Home Office announced in February 2015 that Justice Lowell Goddard from New Zealand had been appointed to head a public inquiry on child abuse in the UK, an inquiry expected to take at least five years. She resigned in August 2016.

Page 23: And there lived another good citizen
Fritzl kept his own daughter Elisabeth in a dungeon below his home for 24 years, while maintaining the appearance of a conventional life above. See below under In Cleveland, Ohio for further comment.

Ray Robinson's novel *Forgetting Zoë* (Heinemann, 2010), developed this recurring theme from a captive's point of view. Set in Newfoundland, it imagines how a little girl had to adapt to eight years of imprisonment: it imagines the process of adaptation to the captor known as the Stockholm syndome. Emma Donohughe's novel Room (Picador, 2010), said to be inspired by the Fritzl case, has a mother and her son both imprisoned in a small room and trying to create a life out of their imprisonment. Maggie Mitchell's novel *Pretty Is* (Orion, 2015), examines through fiction the long-term after-effects on two 12 year-old girls of having been abducted and imprisoned for six weeks in a woodland cabin.

Page 23: And another Austrian abductor

Wolfgang Priklopil abducted a 10-year-old girl, Natascha Kampusch, on her way to school in 1998, and kept her in a cellar for eight years; as soon as she escaped, he committed suicide. The media have not left her alone. A photographic half-page appeared in *The Observer* on 23 August 2009, raising some unanswered questions. Her story was told on Channel 5 TV on 17 February 2010, on 31 May 2012 and on Channel 5 Star on 5 July 2015, on 6 August 2015, 20 December 2015 and 3 April 2016, under the title *Natascha: The Girl in the Cellar*, with Natascha herself in interview showing great composure and no outward sign of bitterness.

Page 24: In Ryazan, in Russia

For kidnapping two 14-year-old girls and imprisoning them for four years, Morkhov was sentenced to 17 years in Siberia. A documentary, *Slaves in the Cellar*, shown on Channel Fiver on 12 February 2011, told their story, how they were rescued by the police and how, remarkably, they survived the ordeal.

Page 24: In a small town called Antioch

Garrido kidnapped his victim when she was 11 and kept her for nearly 20 years. At the trial he was sentenced to 431 years in prison, while his wife was sentenced to 36 years. They had pleaded not guilty. The Judge said that Garrido had 'reinvented slavery'.

Page 25: In Cleveland, Ohio

Castro had pleaded guilty to 937 criminal counts, and BBC

News 24 reported on 4 September 2013 that he had committed suicide in prison. The case of Castro was the starting-point for a full-page feature in *The Observer* on 12 May 2013 under the extended headline, 'It's not just Cleveland: inside the minds of the predators who steal young lives: The case of Ariel Castro has shocked the world- but experts fear many crimes of kidnapping and sexual slavery go undetected. Paul Harris in New York and Ed Pinkington in Cleveland report on the psychology of abuse and violence'.

One of their conclusions was that the experience of childhood abuse by the predator himself was a predisposing factor, while the psychologist Sherry Hamby noted that the desire to control others was expressed by both physical and psychological means. On 27 May 2015, BBC 4 broadcast interviews with two of the three former victims who had decided they were ready to tell their story, giving some detail. The programme was edited by Diana Martin, under the title One World: Kidnapped for a Decade.

Page 26: Now call to mind the night-time cruiser
The crimes of the so-called 'Suffolk Strangler' in 2006 made national news, as did the police search, until Wright was caught using DNA evidence and tried in January 2008. His victims, well known in the London Road area of Ipswich as 'working girls', may have been picked up more than once before being murdered. *Five Daughters*, a three-part drama by Stephen Butchard, was broadcast on BBC1 in April 2010. The intention was to shift attention from the perpetrator, who was not characterised, to the victims and their families. The review in *The Observer* on 2 May 2010 found the drama had great depth though the effect was unsettling. A similar by-product of the Wright case has been the musical *London Road* (where Wright had lived), followed in 2015 by the film directed by Rufus Norris. Musical and film are based not on depiction of the shocking crimes, but

on recorded interviews and reactions drawn from local people who knew the victims or who were affected by the tension of that stressful period. The sung play, 'a story of triumph over fear', to quote from the review in *The Observer*, was performed at the Cottesloe Theatre in 2011 and became a critical success. Innovative dramatisation, semi-operatic treatment of colloquial speech by Adam Cork in a modernised *sprechgesang*, and finally the cinematic interpretation, achieved a community-based work that transcends both the terror and the media frenzy that capitalises on crime.

There is an inspiring finale when the community re-unites in a street party and in a floral hanging-basket competition. The integrity of this work serves as a rebuff to the crime-writing and crime-sensationalising industry, though in this work the issues arising from prostitution, locally and nationally, remain inevitably unresolved.

On Channel 5 TV, 21 April 2010, and repeated on 19 January 2015, a sombre investigative documentary was broadcast featuring research by Professor David Wilson, who deduced that Wright had committed similar crimes earlier in Norwich. Professor Wilson took his investigation of Wright's personal history even further in his series *Killer Psychopaths*, broadcast on Channel 5 TV on 3 March 2015 and repeated on 9 March, deducing that Wright had watched on TV News how the police were responding to his crimes in Ipswich, and had even noted his, Professor Wilson's, response and changed his mode of operation accordingly.

On 28 June 2015 Channel 5 Star broadcast *Killing Spree: Suffolk Strangler*, repeating what had by now become familiar material, itself repeated on 3 April 2016. On 9 August 2015 the same Channel had broadcast *Psychopaths: The Suffolk Strangler*, on the psychology of murderer Steve Wright, with repeats on 3 January and 27 March 2016. *Killer Behind Bars: Steve Wright* was broadcast on 6 December 2015 and 26 May 2016 (not seen). So the media have refocused once again on the archetypal would-be celebrity criminal.

Page 27: Nor could I ever explain

Traditional variations on the nickname 'Jack' occupy four pages of Cassell's *Dictionary of Slang*. When it became clear that the perpetrator of the gruesome Whitechapel murders in 1888 had eluded arrest, he was christened 'Jack the Ripper'. Hoaxers thrived. The 20th-century film industry inherited a convenient audience-magnet for entertainments such as the film *Jack the Ripper* (1958); an exhumation of Thames TV's *Jack the Ripper* (1987) starring Michael Caine, shown on the Drama Channel on 29 March 2016; the TV mini-series *Jack the Ripper* (1988); *The Diary of Jack the Ripper, Beyond Reasonable Doubt*, claiming identification based on a diary; *Jack the Ripper, the Scourge of London*, a collection of documentaries; Channel 5's *Crimes that Shook the World*, including also the crimes of *Sutcliffe; The Ripper from Hell*, abbreviated as *From Hell*, starring Johnny Depp (2001), shown on Movie Mix TV on 17 September 2014, listed as 'Film of the Day', and repeated on Channel 5 Star on 25 and 26 October 2015 and 10 March 2016; *Whitechapel*, another series, about new murders in the same neighbourhood; and *Ripper Street*, a crime drama in eight parts with a fan base so dedicated that when the BBC attempted to close it down, protests from the viewing public led to its resurrection.

A new series, at first in association with Amazon Prime, led to the third series appearing on BBC 1 starting on 31 July 2015. The second episode was particularly disturbing in its content, because of the adoption of material from real life, recorded in some of the cases of abduction highlighted above, in which a young girl was imprisoned for years in a cellar. Linkage with 'true crime' is apparently what the public wants. Enthusiasts may buy the 3-disc DVD box set of the first series of this cult spin-off for only £24.99. But that was only the start. In the world of entertainment, violence and cruelty have a bright commercial future.

The eerie atmosphere of Whitechapel in the fog and the fear of a serial killer at large, in the spirit of the above and under its influence, formed the setting for *Sherlock Holmes – The Case of the Silk Stocking*, a drama for TV starring Rupert Everett. The line drawn between fact and fiction tends to be profitably blurred.

For avid readers, there are the shelves of 'True Crime' in print. In an extended and illustrated review of three new books on crime, carried in *The Observer* on 15 September 2013, Duncan Campbell returned to the cases of Heath and Adams in 1946, with a passing reference to George Orwell's essay *The Decline of the English Murder*. Campbell's general conclusion was that murder, usually reported in individual terms, is also a reflection of society, to which one might add, so is the obsession with murder as reported in the media.

Cold Case: Jack the Ripper, dated 2000, and broadcast on 26 December 2015, named the prime suspect as Aron Kosminski, known to the police and later confined to a mental institution. A re-examination of the evidence by Trevor Marriott, a former Bedfordshire police detective, was broadcast on Channel 5 TV on 25 February 2015, under the title: *Jack the Ripper: New Suspect Revealed*, with repeats on 2 and 3 March. Trevor Marriott concluded that the murderer was a merchant seaman whose crimes in England ceased only because he was executed in the USA for other crimes. But Swedish journalist Christer Holmgren in *Jack the Ripper: the Missing Evidence*, broadcast on 4 June 2015, and repeated on Spike TV Channel on 23 and 27 October 2015, even more plausibly identified his suspect as the witness who claimed he had found the body of the second victim. He was named as Charles Lechmere, a meat delivery driver, and the evidence should in theory bring an end to Rippermania. But there are some in the Ripper industry who would stand to lose if the case were ever solved; *Cold Case* showed the lecturer Donald

Rumbelow entrancing an audience on a Ripper walking tour.

That strange fascination with murder and detection has been exactly placed, colourfully documented and dissected in the series *A Very British Murder* written and introduced by Dr Lucy Worsley and broadcast on BBC 4 TV from 14 February 2014, repeated on the Yesterday channel from 27 October 2015.

Thomas de Quincey was the first to identify the British public as 'murder fanciers' in 1811. The Victorian public turned a series of murderers into celebrity criminals whose crimes acquired even greater notoriety through ballads and newspapers, in one case through theatrical presentation, and through opportunities for the public to visit the scene of the crime. Dickens attended law courts, was a spectator at a public hanging, and saw the opportunity to use serious crime as material for fiction. Dr Worsley traced the beginnings of murder as entertainment to that period, and in the second and third of her series followed her theme through to familiar authors of crime fiction including Dorothy L.Sayers and Graham Greene (quoting *Brighton Rock*, both novel and film), and featuring an interview with the late P.D.James. Dr Worsley paid further tribute to the cinema: Alfred Hitchcock was singled out as a director fascinated by crime, as in his silent film *The Lodger*, subtitled A Story of the London Fog (1926).

In an interview for *The Observer* on November 1, 2015, the crime writer Patricia Cornwell explained how practical research in a laboratory had fed into her work, and how Jack the RIpper had been for her a lifelong obsession. Her *Portrait of a Killer: Jack the Ripper - Case Closed* (2002), attracted controversy when she identified the painter Walter Sickert as the killer. Her sequel was *Chasing the Ripper* (2014).

The responsibility of the media for feeding the same fascination was discussed in a thoughtful piece in *The Observer* on 14 October 2014. The extended headline ran: 'We are all to blame for media scrum at horror crime scenes, says Gyllenhaall: The actor's new film, *Nightcrawler*, is a dark satire of TV's obsession with breaking news'. The piece focused on press photographers who make money from images of car crashes and their victims; another aim of Gyllenhaal's film 'was to show how the media preys on people's fears … (with) news reports that lean heavily on violent, graphic images, with brief narratives to invoke drama and excitement...'. The film's writer-director links these fears in America to the demand for ownership of guns. There are careers to be shaped and profits to be made by the encouragement of fear.

Throughout the above, sensationalism predominates. On a different level, the Ripper-influence entered into serious literature, music and film. Franz Wedekind's *Erdgeist* (1895) inspired Alban Berg's opera *Lulu* (1929-35), as well as G.W.Pabst's silent film *Pandora's Box*, also known as Lulu (1929), starring Louise Brooks. There are shocks, but these are contained within the conventions of melodrama.

Part III: In human conflict

Page 31: Alexander, *336* BC
In his short lifetime (356-323 BC), Alexander the Great (Alexander III or Alexander of Macedonia) built an extensive empire in the Middle East by military means, but the empire was relatively shortlived. While he was alive and, even more, posthumously, in the absence of clear evidence, the legend of his invincibility encouraged romantic admiration and hero-worship. For the Alexander of legend see the handsome volume by Alan Filden and Joanna Fletcher, *Alexander the Great, Son of the Gods* (Duncan Baird, for the J.Paul Getty Museum, 2001).

But this was a record that always needed to be set straight. See Paul Cartledge's reassessment, *Alexander the Great: the Hunt for a New Past* (Macmillan, 2014) and the long entry in *The Encylopaedia Britannica.* The sacking of Thebes and the massacre of its inhabitants was not his first 'victory' but it was the earliest sign of the brutal campaigns to come. For a similar perspective on Julius Caesar, see Mary Beard's *SPQR, A History of Ancient Rome* (Profile, 2015), pp. 284-5.

Page 33: The Massacre of the Innocents 4 BC (?)
The Biblical story of the Massacre of the Holy Innocents (Matthew, 2.16) has never been authentically dated to Jesus's lifetime, nor is there agreement about the dates for Herod the Great, whose death occurred probably about 4 BC. See Diarmaid MacCulloch, *A History of Christianity* (Allen Lane, 2009), pp.78-9, for a succinct deconstruction of the confusing Biblical time-line. Peake's *Commentary on the Bible* (1992) takes the reader and student into 'Matthew's way of adapting prophetic texts', and back to Exodus, with Israel in Egypt, the Tenth Plague, and the Passover, quoting Frazer, who refers to the Paschal ritual: 'the one thing that looms clear through the haze of this weird tradition is the memory of a great massacre of the first-born.'

The *Commentary* continues: 'While not unique in antiquity, the cruelty of Herod had become proverbial even in Rome. But the massacre is not mentioned by Josephus, who tells about many of the ferocities of Herod' (p.772). It is the Biblical confusion that is responsible for mis-dating the legendary massacre; see Exodus 11.5. and 12.29: 'And it came to pass that at midnight the Lord smote all the first-born in the land of Egypt...'

Pieter Brueghel the Elder (c.1525-1569) presciently and pointedly transferred the Biblical story or stories to a contemporary setting in the Netherlands, giving it a contemporary relevance and impact, much as Stanley Spencer transferred religious subjects to Cookham in the 1930s. But the same can be said of other examples in the long tradition of religious painting.

Brueghel's painting *The Massacre of the Innocents* has been dated 1566. Two versions exist; of the several copies that have been made, one is in the Kunsthistorisches Museum in Vienna, and the other in Her Majesty's collection at Windsor Castle. But while the latter copy was in the possession of the Holy Roman Emperor Rudolph II, between 1604-1621, the stark details of the massacre were discreetly over-painted and its impact greatly diminished (unlike the Viennese version). It passed into the collection of our own Charles II. During conservation work in 1988 the restorers decided to retain the over-painting, arguably committing a gross injustice to Brueghel and his artistic vision.

The irony is that while the present piece describes the soldier swinging a child by its arm as if swinging a bird by its wing, as in the original, the Windsor Castle version defeats Brueghel's intention by nonsensically overpainting the child with an unconvincing bird! Enough said. See Manfred Sellink, *Brueghel* (Ludion, 2007). For the most detailed analysis of the multiple narratives in this painting, visit https://www.royal collection.org. uk or search under Royal Collection Trust or under *The Massacre of the Innocents.*

Spain in Brueghel's lifetime has been described as the most powerful monarchy in the world. The Netherlands were ruled from Spain by the catholic King Philip II who, following his accession in 1555, authorised a harsh régime and persecution of the Netherland Protestants. The campaign was led by his ruthless governor, the Duke of Alva. The Duke is said to be represented in Brueghel's painting by the grim bearded figure in black, and on horseback, heading his troop of German mercenaries in full armour. Tim Marlow, when discussing Brueghel in his *Great Artists* series, accepted this identification (A *Seventh Art* Production for Channel 5, 2001). J.E.Neale's *Queen Elizabeth 1* (Cape, 1934) keeps the Duke of Alva in view in the Elizabethan context.

For a comparison with another artist's visionary imagination, see *The Massacre at Chios* in the Louvre, painted by Eugène Delacroix (1793-1863). This is an overly theatrical but nevertheless powerful impression of the massacre by Ottoman troops of 20,000 Greeks on the neutral island of Chios, during the Greek War of Independence in 1822.

Page 36: Jerusalem: The First Crusade, 1099 AD
Plentiful documentation of the First Crusade has survived, enabling some commentators to give an almost blow-by-blow account of the final siege and capture of the Holy City after the expedition that had taken the crusaders three costly and exhausting years. Commenting on the 'disconnect' between Christianity and the slaughter at Jerusalem, leading to the pious and ecstatic thanksgiving in the Church of the Holy Sepulchre, Karen Armstrong, in *Fields of Blood: Religion and the History of Violence* (Bodley Head, 2014), goes to the heart of the matter: 'The holy war and the ideology that inspired it represented a complete denial of the pacifist strain in Christianity' (p.192).

Karen Armstrong summarises Jesus's injunction to 'love your enemies' (p.126) and quotes the famous 'turn the other cheek' passage in Luke Ch.6, vv.27-31. But if taken with other key passages including Matthew Ch.5, vv.9-12 (Matthew also copies the 'other cheek' saying), and vv. 43-44, and Romans Ch.12, vv.

17-21, and Ch.13 vv.9-10, and most significantly, the last hours of Jesus, her expression 'pacifist strain' in Christianity looks like an understatement, or a sideways shift from what Christianity was meant to be into what it later became. The famous sayings are not secondary admonitions. They are primary teachings expressing core principles as the basis for radically changing the way people live. The 'holy war' and the ideology that inspired it was a staggering dismissal of central Christian teaching. Military historians tend to regard the expedition as ultimately successful, as if the end justifies the means, however debatable that may be. Historians may turn aside from the action to give an account of the conversion of Christianity from the fourth century onwards into a new *modus vivendi* with the state; see Thomas Asbridge, *The First Crusade, A New History* (Simon and Shuster, 2005) pp.23, 27, 37, noting that Pope Gregory VII went further in proposing a papal army, and the same author's *The Crusades: The War for the Holy Land* (2010), pp.12-14.

Dr Asbridge provides a gripping narrative. But Christopher Tyerman in *God's War* (Allen Lane, 2006) gives greater weight to the spiritual and moral issues. In his opening chapter, under the heading *War, the Bible and Classical Theory* (pp.28-57), Tyerman notes the 'plasticity' of Augustine's theory of the 'just war', while discussing the 'prehistory' of the First Crusade. It is a plasticity that is glibly exploited even in modern times. On 3 and 4 February 2016, on BBC4, Dr Asbridge presented *The Crusades: A Timewatch Guide,* or a review of 70 years of historiography, and drew attention to the pogroms of Jews before and during the First Crusade, and to the limited interest shown by Arab historians. For the rich, colourful and contentious history of the Holy City in depth, see Simon Sebag Montefiore's *Jerusalem* (Weidenfeld and Nicolson, 2011), although his presentation to camera on TV of the carnage of 1099 was criticised in *A Timewatch Guide* for sensationalism.

For contemporary and near-contemporary accounts, a primary source is *The Alexiad,* by the Emperor Alexius's daughter Anna Comnena, trans. E.R.A.Sewter (London, 1969). Karen Armstrong and others refer to the first-hand account by Raymond of Aguiler, ed. and trans. by August C.Krey, in *The First Crusade: The Accounts of Eyewitnesses and Participants* (Princeton and London, 1921). Works consulted: Conor Kostick, *The Siege of Jerusalem, Crusade and Conquest in 1099* (Continuum, 2009); *Holy Warriors, a Modern History of the Crusades* by Jonathan Phillips, Professor of Crusading History, Royal Holloway, University of London (Random House, 2009); Michael Foss, *People of the First Crusade, the Truth about the Christian-Muslim War Revealed* (Arcade, 1997, 2011); Diarmaid MacCulloch, *A History of Christianity*, pp. 383-4 (Allen Lane, 2009); Judith Herrin, *Byzantium, The Surprising life of a Medieval Empire* (Penguin, 2007); and Philip Sherrard, *Byzantium* (Time-Life, 1966). Prof. Phillips' *Holy Warriors* contains an extensive Bibliography giving sources and secondary material. In Part 3 of his BBC4 series on *The Normans,* broadcast on 7 April 2015, Professor Robert Bartlett explained how 'the first Norman knights were enticed South, united in their lust for gain', winning control of Southern Italy and Sicily, before being caught up in the First Crusade. There were no reconstructions in this programme, just blurry images and stirring music. Prof. Bartlett described the culmination of the expedition as 'a massacre that the Muslims never forgot or forgave'.

In the present narrative, Raymond's titles as Count of Toulouse and Lord of St Gilles are used interchangeably. Wealthy leader of the southern Franks, Raymond was already on good terms with Alexius. He is seen here as the most complex of the leaders. Though religious, he becomes complicit in extreme violence. With so much detail about Raymond's participation already available, it may seem unnecessary to add any more on the imaginative level, but the leaders of the expedition had greater means than most to enable them to survive, and one can deduce that Raymond had the support of an *entourage* brought with him as would befit a Frankish Count. It may seem that Raymond's patronage of the minstrel's song, with its literary and musical connotations, will seem too early. Soon enough, the itinerant minstrels would become differentiated from the troubadours, who would depend on courtly patronage. But Raymond was well-placed for the precursors of the troubadours. He was also well placed to hear embryonic versions of the *chansons de geste*. Though the Age of Chivalry had barely dawned, Raymond was in a privileged position to register change.

Nevertheless, the introduction of *The Song of Roland* here is entire supposition. No original text of the *Song* survives and the 'Digby 23' MS in the Bodleian Library in Oxford, edited in 1837, is only 'a copy of a copy of a copy'. As the text reads today, *Roland* is too late for Raymond. But *Roland* is thought to have originated early enough, during the period 1064-1120, for Raymond to have heard it in an early version. The present narrative imagines Raymond in his princely court having heard, and having been impressed by, a minstrel or a courtly poet-composer singing an early version of *The Song of Roland*. For *chanson de geste* and *minstrel* (a term of convenience), see the entries in *The New Grove Dictionary of Music and Musicians*. Though the military *milieu* of the First Crusade was not the place for the troubadours, every court needed its entertainers, musicians, minstrels and poets to interpret the past as well as the present (this is to discount the necromancers, magicians, soothsayers and faux-physicians). It was a time for epic and narrative rather than lyric verse.

Roland provides a connection with the legacy of the civilised and cultured travelling court of Charlemagne (742-814), the warrior king of the Franks, who established what eventually became the Holy Roman Empire, and who had similarly been engaged in fighting infidels. However, though Count Raymond travelled with his personal retinue including steward, servants and priest, no one has previously suggested that he brought a minstrel with him, or that he identified with the legendary Roland, as he could, and might, have done.

For a helpful introduction, see Howard S. Robinson, *The Song of Roland* (Dent, 1972). For a translation, see Janet Shirley, *Song of Roland* (1996). Ms Shirley notes that 'Durendal' may derive from an Arabic word meaning 'Shining, brilliant', and translates 'Veuillantil' as 'Wideawake', for which one might also suggest 'Vigilant'. A sidelong glance at another great sword, Siegmund's 'Nothung' in Wagner's *Die Walküre,* Act I, underlines the point that in an age of magic and superstition, Roland's 'Veuillantil' was not inanimate but a living thing. Its special virtue was indicated by the hilt, embedded with holy relics and decorated with jewels. The borrowing from *Roland* also helps to colour in a part of the background of life and thought that is missing from the military history of the First Crusade. Ms Shirley comments appositely that by the early 12th century, 'the Franks were certain that they were God's own special combat troops'. During the First Crusade the episode of the Holy Lance highlights the powerful presence of magic and superstition driven by faith. The parallels between the conflict in which Roland is engaged and the crusaders' conflict with Muslims are striking. In *Roland* the hero experiences defeat, and the parallel may be drawn with Count Raymond's sense of failure when his rival Duke Godfrey takes Jerusalem and enjoys right of conquest.

A note on jousting: the first recorded date of a jousting tournament is 1066 (no connection with the battle of Hastings), giving time for this extreme sport to reach southern France. But jousting at this stage of its development would have been more like military training than the elaborate courtly spectacles of the late Middle Ages.

Page 63: Cathars, 1209 and 1244
In the 11th and 12th centuries these 'True Christians' were based in Albi in southwest France. They were originally known as Albigensians and later labelled 'Cathars' as a term of abuse. Condemned by the Catholic Church as heretics, the Cathars were essentially a peace-loving separatist sect under severe

persecution for their unorthodox beliefs. The first armed crusade against the Cathars, known as the Albigensian Crusade, ended in the assault on Béziers on 2 July 1209. The second ended in the siege of Montségur between 1243-4. On both occasions a small group of Cathars had uncharacteristically broken a principle and killed one of their persecutors. In each case the crime was met not with a trial but with massive indiscriminate reprisals, in which the Church collaborated with the state.

The activity of the Inquisition had played a key part in precipitating the tragedy at Montségur. For a summary accessible to the general reader, see Jonathan Phillips, *Holy Warriors*, Ch.8, and for further details see his Bibliography. Part of the *Manual for Inquisitors*, dated 1245-6, is translated in W.L.Wakefield, *Heresy, Crusade and Inquisition in Southern France, 1100-1250* (London, 1974). It is difficult to see how the 20 questions listed could have been handled in this exact form because each question implies that the person being interrogated already knows what is meant by heresy. There were even slight shifts in the accepted definition as obscurities were progressively explained. So it has not been possible simply to insert these questions into the present piece. The modern reader could be even more baffled. So the questions built into the present piece are a composite of what was understood at the time and what the modern reader might make of it.

On 13 October 2014, under the ominous title Inquisition, a semi-dramatic account of the terror it inspired was presented, in sensational style, on the Yesterday TV channel . Medieval Dead, on 7 December 2015, presented the archaeological evidence. *In A History of Christianity* pages 404-405, Diarmaid MacCulloch comments that Pope Innocent III 'did in the end blanch at the indiscriminate violence that he had unleashed.' In reference to the Cathars, Professor MacCulloch enlarged on his commentary in *A History of Christianity* when reviewing R.J.Moore's *The War on Heresy* (Profile, 2012). The review, which appeared in *The Times Literary Supplement* on 4 July 2012 under the title *Burning the Cathars*, explains and discusses the origins of Catharism as emerging from a dualist view of creation and the cosmos. The background is the period of reform in the Western Church, to which Pope Gregory VII (1073-85) gave prominence, the same Pope who inspired Urban II to launch the First Crusade. (See the piece in this sequence preceding Cathars, under the title *Jerusalem: The First Crusade*). For Professor MacCulloch's review of R.J.Moore's work, visit the internet, as well as for an even more detailed survey entitled *Cathars and Cathar Beliefs in the Languedoc*, including Cathar Wars, the Catholic Church, Cathar Inquisition, Cathar Castles and the Cathar Legacy. But the overall verdict on this episode is that the Cathars had arrived at a truer vision of the Christian life than those who denounced them as heretics and zealously burned them to death, conveniently seizing their land.

Although the memorial is at Montségur, it appears that some of the Cathars may have been taken elsewhere to be burned.

Page 72: Saint Bartholomew's Day, 24 August 1572
See J.E.Neale, *Queen Elizabeth 1* (Cape, 1934) , Ch.14, for an unambiguous account, as Catherine places herself in a dilemma and a crisis with international repercussions.

This is the same story as that dramatised by Christopher Marlowe in *The Massacre at Paris* (1592) though the surviving text of that play is incomplete. A summary of the historical background may be found in M. Frohnsdorff and K. Pickering's *Great Neglected Speeches from the Elizabethan Stage* (Pen Press, 2010). Marlowe is credited with the first use of the word 'massacre' in English. D.W.Griffiths included the St Bartholomew's Day Massacre as part 3 of his silent epic *Intolerance* (1916), though more relevant to the history of film than to history on film. Gabriel García Márquez includes the massacre as one of 'the hideous slaughters of European history' in *The General in his Labyrinth*, 1989 (Penguin, 2008).

Catherine de Médicis came from the Florentine family of

whom the best known is Lorenzo di' Médicis, aka Lorenzo the Magnificent, ruler of Florence and extravagant patron of the arts. Catherine was Regent of France from 1560-74. In Marlowe's complex plot, Catherine is incriminated in the massacre. If Marlowe, like Shakespeare, is deferring to the Tudor view of history, then he is writing Protestant propaganda, and in so doing has done an injustice to Catherine. If Catherine intended to bring about a reconciliation between Catholics and Protestants, then we are left with the question of how the fatal plot was hatched without her knowledge. Could she have been distracted by the wedding preparations and festivities? Modern writers tend to place the responsibility for plotting and carrying out the massacre on the Catholic lords in her council. There is a sidelight on the attention given to the entertainment provided for the guests: in 1564, with discernment and musical insight, Catherine had ordered 30 violins from Andrea Amati in Cremona. She would ensure that the musical entertainment for the festivities in 1572, including the dancing at court would, fittingly, be of the highest quality.

The massacre at Paris in 1572 is not the only massacre at Paris that deserves to be remembered. Wordsworth drew on the 'September massacres' of 1792 during the French Revolution in his autobiographical poem *The Prelude* (written and revised 1798-1805/1850), a shocking episode when Marat and a gang of assassins entered the city's prisons and killed hundreds of prisoners.

In 1792 the actress, playwright, novelist and editor Elizabeth Inchbald responded to the same events with her play *Massacre* (the action is mainly off-stage), but in the prevailing political climate in England (see under '*Peterloo*' below) felt able only to circulate the play among her radical friends. The play had to wait till 2009 for its English première. Benjamin Britten drew from Wordsworth's *The Prelude* (Book 10, ll. 54-77, adapted) in his *Nocturne* (1958), interpreting the passage in music. The massacre in the prisons is distinct from The Terror of 1793-4. These events deserve a detailed background that is not possible to give here.

The same applies to the February Revolution, also known as the 'June Days', in Paris in 1848, when General Louis-Eugène Cavaignac, leading the National Guard, turned artillery on rebels, killing an estimated 1,500, after which 12,000 were arrested and deported; or the brief uprising in 1851 following Louis-Napoleon's *coup d'état,* with Victor Hugo among the insurgents, following the dissolution of the National Assembly, during which several hundred demonstrators were killed by D'Allonville's cavalry and 27,000 arrested; or the massacre carried out by General Gaffinet in order to suppress the Communards during the revolutionary experiment in 1871, in which an estimated 15,000 Parisians were killed and thousands more imprisoned or exiled.

Page 73: Drogheda, 10 September 1649

From the abundance of material on Cromwell and the New Model Army, especially during his campaign in Ireland, see the key quotations from Cromwell's letters in Tristram Hunt, Ch.XI, *The English Civil War at First Hand* (Weidenfeld and Nicolson, 2002), and also Micheal O Siochru's *God's Executioner: Oliver Cromwell and the Conquest of Ireland* (Faber, 2008).

Page 75: Glencoe, 13 February 1692

John Prebble's *Glencoe, The Story of the Massacre* (Secker & Warburg, 1966), disentangles the existing animosities between the clans, expressed in their ancient feuds, raiding and cattle-stealing, and the secret links between John Campbell of Breadalbane and the supporters of the exiled Catholic James II in France. Campbell was an astute double-dealer, simultaneously accepting together with other chiefs of the clans the £12,000 bribe from King William III for declaring loyalty to the English Crown, while supporting James. Scottish sympathisers of James awaited news of an invasion force supported by Louis XIV of France, but news of its cancellation and James's advice to sign tipped the scales and all the chiefs excepting Iain MacDonald signed the declaration of loyalty to William. News, having been maliciously delayed, reached Iain only just before the deadline. He set off to Fort William, wrongly, had to take the longer journey to Inverary and missed the deadline, but signed in good faith. The story of how his name was deliberately deleted from the list of signatures that were actually accepted led to a tragic outcome.

Sir John Dalrymple, the Master of Stair, later Earl of Stair, was the King's Secretary of State for Scotland. Stair is a small estate in the District of Kyle, Ayrshire. The arrogant Master of Stair had no time for the MacDonalds. He sought to teach the MacDonalds a lesson and subsequent events exposed his vengeful nature. The Master's instructions, signed by King William, implicated the King himself in the massacre that followed: *If M'Kean of Glencoe, and that tribe, can be well separated from the rest, it will be a proper vindication of the public justice to extirpate that sept* (clan) *of thieves'*. The instructions were carried out by the Earl of Argyll's Regiment under the command of Captain Robert Campbell of Glenlyon.

Following a fortnight of traditional hospitality given to the soldiers billeted at Glencoe, with Highland Games and entertainment, 38 members of the MacDonald clan were killed by the soldiers, acting on secret orders, though two of the sons of the Chief of the clan escaped and later returned to Glencoe. Soon afterwards the King discharged the Master of Stair from responsibility.

A Parliamentary Commission held three years later led to a Report, published in 1703: *The Massacre of Glenco, being a true narrative of the Barbarous Murther of the Glenco-men in the Highlands of Scotland, by way of military execution, on 13th February 1692.* But responsibility was partly covered up. A second Inquiry two years later did reveal the truth and was a considerable embarrassment to William III, implicating him in effect as having committed an act of treason against his own people. No one ever stood trial for the massacre.

A poem in Gaelic on Glencoe by Bhard Mhucanach (The

Muck Bard) was published in 1776. A well-researched drama-documentary, *Glencoe*, made for BBC Scotland and directed and produced by Craig Hunter, was made in 2007, repeated on 19 January 2015 on the TV Channel *Yesterday* and also on 2 September. A play by Adrian Bean entitled *Murder under Trust: The Massacre at Glencoe*, and covering the same ground, was broadcast on Radio 4 on 16 August, 2014.

Page 77: Culloden, 16 April 1746

John Prebble's *Culloden* (Secker & Warburg, 1961) ranks alongside his *Glencoe* (above). Visitors to the battle-site may purchase Iain Cameron Taylor's *Culloden, A Guidebook to the Battlefield, with the Story of the Battle, the Events leading to it and the Aftermath* (The National Trust for Scotland, 1965). Robert Burns on one of his four Highland journeys in 1787 passed through Culloden Moor, and made the following laconic note in his Journal: *"Reflections on the field of battle"*. Burns clearly did have some reflections at the time.

But as Ian McIntyre points out in his *Robert Burns, A Life* (Constable, 1995), 'Burns did not expand on these reflections in either verse or prose'. Burns was a Jacobite and on the same journey had already passed Killiecrankie, site of a Jacobite victory, 'but his muse had failed to inspire him there.' In his poems, Burns refers several times to Wallace, as a heroic figure of the past, so his silence on Killiecrankie, though he composed verses to the tune K*illiecrankie*, and his near-silence on Culloden, remain a mystery. Burns's *Ballad on the American War,* in Scottish dialect, weaving the leading American historical figures into a narrative, is set to the tune *Killiecrankie!*

An outstanding documentary reconstruction, *Culloden* (1964), was made by Peter Watkins for the BBC, using amateur actors and extras from Inverness. On more traditional lines the film *Culloden, 1746,* directed by Graham Holloway (1994), traces the arrival of the Young Pretender and his failure to attract sufficient support from the Scots, shown as leaderless and divided, while the English are obviously better organised and kitted out. The Jacobites, ill-equipped, march cold and hungry towards inevitable defeat by the well-drilled Redcoats.

To make matters worse, the Young Pretender lacks charisma and relies entirely on the dwindling attachment of the Scots towards his father. But a sub-plot involving the tragic division and demise of one family caught up in the disaster (the family of Alastair Campbell) is well worked out, even to its bitter end on the misty battlefield. A two-part documentary on *The Stuarts in Exile*, shown on BBC4 on 27 October and 3 November 2015, presented by Dr Clare Jackson, explained lucidly how the 1715 rebellion was bungled and how the '45 failed because of insufficient support on the ground. Dr Jackson followed through to the Stuarts' sorry end abroad.

The present piece may not make up for the omission by Robert Burns, but is based on real-life reflections during a visit to the Culloden battle-site.

Page 79: 'Peterloo' , 16 August 1819
For a political, social and economic perspective on the troubled post-Napoleonic War period, see John W. Derry, *Reaction and Reform,1793-1868 (*Blandford, 1963), as well as the same author's rehabilitation of Sidmouth's colleague in the Liverpool administration, *Castlereagh* (Allen Lane, 1976), and *Politics in the Age of Fox, Pitt and Liverpool: Continuity and Transformation* (Macmillan, 1990).

Details of the massacre and its aftermath are to be found in Joyce Marlow's *The Peterloo Massacre* (Rapp and Whiting, 1969), and elsewhere. For the contentious blue plaque and its red replacement by the Manchester City Council, refer to Appendix, p.205, and the internet.

It is important to appreciate that in this period the role of government did not extend to responsibility for social welfare, or even to the alleviation of distress. The administration, centred in London, had little knowledge of the problems caused by the growing manufacturing industries in the north. The creation of new wealth and the tension between wages and profits were features of an economy that was not understood and was in any case out of control. The social and economic problems of industrialisation have been analysed in depth: see bibliographies in the works cited above. Arthur Bryant, in *The Age of Elegance* (Collins, 1950) argues that measures were available through progressive taxation and fiscal planning that could have transformed the economy, and could have reduced hardships at the level of starvation and degradation for the common people (see Ch.11 and pp.358-9). But the poor were already taxed and, having no resources, were at the mercy of the rise and fall of rents and prices. There existed a widespread philosophy that placed responsibility for solving problems, whatever they were, on the individual - convenient for those with inherited wealth - which was a failure to see that there is such a thing as society. Visionary thinkers were in short supply. All that those in distress could do was to send in massive petitions to the House of Commons.

There are several reasons for looking again at the 'Peterloo' episode and the period in which it took place. To name only two: it embraces the constitutional re-alignment of the monarchy and parliament, leading to the alignment of the present day; and it features the activity of popular movements demanding reform, taking place in the troubled aftermath of the Napoleonic Wars, with the fear of Jacobinism becoming almost a paranoia. Any leader of a popular movement for reform could be labelled as a dangerous revolutionary, giving rise to reactionary measures imposed by a government that wasn't in the habit of listening. This is already well known, but the present piece is equally concerned to highlight the damage to justice and trust caused by the blunders of the forces of law and order, both during the event at St Peter's Fields on 16 August, 1819, and in the subsequent morally bankrupt attempt to gloss over the killings. One irony that the Liverpool adminstration did not live long enough to grasp, was that reform would not weaken central government; it would, in the end, strengthen it.

It is particularly distasteful to read in the official biography by G.Pellew, *The Life and Correspondence of the Right Honourable Henry Addington, First Viscount Sidmouth* (London, 1847, vol.3), how the biographer drip-feeds the reader with judgemental language in order to create an England on the verge of revolution. Those protesting against economic hardship or calling for an extended franchise are always the Mob. (The solitary surviving banner from 'Peterloo', though faded, carries the word 'Vote'). Their meetings are by their very nature seditious. Those speaking at meetings are conspirators. According to an address to the Magistrates at the quarter sessions at Salford, 'the restless spirit of sedition' indicated 'an approaching effort to involve the country in the horrors of a revolution.' In Sidmouth's words, 'To hold an inquiry would be inconsistent with the clearest principles of public justice.' To the modern reader, this tendentious form of reasoning reveals arrogance, self-delusion, and a readiness to use lies for political purposes.

The catchy ironic coinage "Peter Loo" appeared first in *The Manchester Observer* for Saturday 21 August, 1919, and 'just-asses' is taken from a vituperative satirical piece that appeared in the next edition on Saturday 28 August. The headline, AN IMPORTANT COMMUNICATION TO THE PEOPLE OF ENGLAND, was effectively undercut by copy that followed. Sidmouth made sure that the editor would be suitably punished; he was sentenced to a year in prison. 'Proceedings at Manchester' is Sidmouth's weasel euphemism for the massacre, and the words 'salutary lesson to modern reformers' are Sidmouth's own. Major Trafford, so warmly congratulated by the Prince Regent, had not led the Manchester and Salford Yeomanry cavalry charge to arrest Orator Hunt; he had in fact delegated the task to his second-in-command, Hugh Henry Birley, who took the blame. But no inquiry was held either in London or in Manchester. The magistrates tried unsuccessfully to prove that the assembly had been riotous and that Hunt had incited the crowd to violence. The coroner at the inquest refused to hear evidence to the contrary.

The cartoonists lost no opportunity to depict and exploit the madness of the cavalry charge. Cruickshank in his first satirical cartoon showed the Yeomen on horseback waving not sabres but battleaxes dripping with blood, like the axes of executioners. His second shows the Yeomen with sabres, acting with the same disregard for life. Outraged lampoons were printed and Part II of the present piece is intended to follow that tradition of lampoonery. The historian Amanda Vickery, in *Suffragettes Forever! The Story of Women and Power* (presented on BBC 2, 25 February 2015) argued that women in the crowd at Peterloo were singled out as targets because their presence challenged male supremacy, as the cartoons would appear to show, but it is not clear how the Yeomanry could have had time and space to be selective; it seems more likely that in the hurly-burly the indiscriminate use of violence would have caused the greatest harm to the most defenceless.

It should be added that the magistrates had a small army standing by to put down an insurrection, had there been one. There were 1,500 troops mounted and on foot, out of sight, including the 15th Hussars, several squadrons of the 88th Foot, and a detachment of the Royal Horse Artillery manning two long six-pounders (ready for an even greater massacre), as well as 400 men of the Cheshire Yeomanry and 200 of the Manchester and Salford Yeomanry, of whom 120 were used, together with 400 Special Constables. It was all an example, one might say, of overkill. (*See* Ch.15, *The Peterloo Massacre*).

Sidmouth had already decided to suppress the truth when he requested a letter from the Prince Regent approving the actions of the Manchester magistrates. The Prince Regent was if anything even more out of touch with the condition of his people and their problems, though facing hostility on some of his appearances in public. He lived in his own self-indulgent bubble. But obtaining the letter was a deft move on Sidmouth's part: he caused Royalty to connive in a *suppressio veri* at the same time as obtaining blanket approval for measures yet to be announced. For contemporary impressions, caricatures and some flattering portraits of George, see Christopher Hibbert's *George IV: Regent and King, 1811-1830* (Allen Lane, 1973). In his essay *George IV: A Sketch (History Today,* 2005, Vol.55, 10) Kenneth Baker presents the monarch's merits as well as his demerits.

Page 85: The Battleship Potemkin, *1905*

Sergei Eisenstein's film *The Battleship Potemkin* (1926, silent) is a fictive dramatisation of a mutiny that did occur in the Russian fleet at Sevastopol in the Crimea in 1905, transferred to the Black Sea port of Odessa. It is not a documentary, it is a representation of what '1905' stands for, in a story of the people (the proletariat) rising against the autocratic rule of Tsar Nicholas II, who governed without a prime minister and who was believed by the peasantry to have been appointed by God. The story is structured retrospectively from the angle of a communist who believed fully in the Bolshevik Revolution of 1917.

The incidents that make up the film have a symbolic rather than a literal meaning, so that the repressive action of the Tsar's Cossacks, transferred by Eisenstein to the Odessa steps for their cinematic effect and dramatic potential, stands for every other repressive measure carried out in the name of the Tsar in 1905. Not least, it stands for the massacre on 9 January 1905 of hundreds of the thousands of unarmed striking workers led by Father Georgy Gapon, who were marching in procession in St Petersburg to present a petition to the Tsar in the Winter Palace. Their motivation was economic but becoming increasingly political. After these events, not surprisingly, the Tsar left the Winter Palace for good.

Demands from the working class and the intelligentsia for representation and reform were met by the Tsar with empty promises and censorship. It is not possible to convey here the complexity of the struggle to articulate these demands under a reactionary and repressive régime. The strikes and demonstrations of 1905 fizzled out and there was no revolution. But in communist mythology the events of 1905 became the precursors of the revolution that occurred 12 years later, in which the action of the sailors of the *Aurora* in firing a symbolic blank shot towards the Winter Palace, in 1917, became the action of heroes remembered today. The *Aurora* is still moored in an honoured position on the River Neva. A postscript on 1905 and what it stands for: music-lovers will not have missed Shostakovich's Symphony No 11 in G minor Op.103, first performed in 1957, and subtitled *1905*.

For a holistic study of Russia in which these and allied events are placed in context, see Orlando Figes, *Natasha's Dance, A Cultural History of Russia* (Penguin, 2002). For Eisenstein and *Potemkin,* see p.459 and the Bibliography which includes studies of Soviet cinema. Orlando Figes is Professor of History at Birkbeck College, University of London. See also Bernard Pares, *A History of Russia* (Methuen, 1926/1955) and other standard sources.

Page 87: Armenia, 1915-16
The uprooting and dispersal of the Armenians, remembered here, was the culmination a long series of violent attacks on Armenian communities, as Diarmaid MacCulloch points out in *A History of Christianity (*pp.277, 854-55, 920-1 and 926-7). The Turkish authorities appear to have imposed an embargo on information that has lasted till today. In *Archduke Franz Ferdinand Lives!* (2014), Richard Ned Lebow sees the Armenian dispersal and slaughter as a precedent that set the scene for the 20th century; it influenced future dictators by demonstrating how to dehumanise whole populations by means of 'ethnic cleansing', before moving on to genocide. On 12 March 2015, Pope Francis named these actions as 'the first genocide of the 20th century'. However, David Olusoga writing in *The Observer* on 19 March 2015 pointed out that the extermination of most of the Herero tribe by the German occupation in Namibia had that distinction, having taken place between 1904-1909.

In a wide survey of the persecution of Christians, with the title *Kill the Christians*, broadcast on BBC 2 TV on 15 and 16 April 2015, Jane Corbin (both producer and presenter) drew on documentary evidence of the Armenian genocide as a background to present-day persecution by Islamic militants. In *Our World: Remembering the Armenian Massacres,* broadcast on BBC News 24 on 25 April 2015, descendants of some of those expelled from Armenia returned to the ruined sites where Armenians once lived and worshipped and to towns where Armenian communities had once flourished, and where the few who admit to Armenian ancestry are afraid to admit that they are Christians, with one exception: those in the centre of Istanbul. A Turkish historian was interviewed; he claimed that what had taken place in 1915 was 'techir', or 'relocation', not genocide. A film entitled *The Cut* (not seen), by the German-Turkish director Fatih Akin, and covering the aftermath of the Armenian genocide on an epic scale, was released in 2014.

Page 89: Amritsar, 13 April 1919
See John Keay's *A History of India* (HarperCollins, 2000), in which the author notes the stirrings of the movement for independence, including the activities of M.K.Gandhi, prior to the massacre at Amritsar in the Punjab on 13 April 1919.

The mutiny of native Indian soldiers under British officers in 1857-8 had led to rebellious disturbances and killings, a history that formed the attitudes of many British soldiers, as well as of some of the administrators in the civil service, towards the native population at large. Colonial relationships remained uneasy and could not even begin to be reconciled until, in 1947, India achieved Independence. In 1919, Gandhi, unlike the rebels in the Indian Mutiny, was pursuing the principles of non-violence. To some British colonialists it was all the same: mass resistance by the governed was an ever-present danger to the continuance of the British Empire, and in this spirit the Rowlatt Bills of 1918 imposed emergency powers (as we would say, suspending *Magna*

Carta) in peacetime.

Acknowledgements to *The Dictionary of National Biography* (2004), Vol. 17 p. 489, for details repeated here. Three days before the massacre, a mob had rioted and killed five Englishmen. Following Rowlatt, the Lieutenant-Governor of the Punjab, Sir Michael O'Dwyer, authorised Brigadier-General Sir Reginald Dyer to enforce a ban on public meetings. Sir Reginald marched a force of 90 Gurkhas and Baluchi troops into the Jallianwalla Bagh, a walled enclosure near the Golden Temple, with only one exit. Sir Reginald could claim that he was acting under authorisation. But his failure to give warning before opening fire was held against him, as was the absence of any attempt to give aid to the casualties. The Governor of India reluctantly appointed a Committee of Inquiry, at which Sir Reginald appeared only as a witness. Meeting in October 1919, the Committee heard that 1,650 rounds had been fired, killing 379 Indians and wounding 1,200 men, women and children. No aid was given to the wounded. Sir Reginald justified his actions on the grounds that he had prevented a general rebellion. As the news crept out there was an international outcry.

And so, far from helping to preserve British rule over India, Sir Reginald Dyer's action helped in the long term to ensure Indian independence. His 'crawling' order exposed his underlying racism. After his long military career, culminating in Amritsar, Sir Reginald was forced to resign from the Indian army. He returned to England, where he was rewarded with a donation of £28,000 from the public, and died in 1927. He was given an unofficial state funeral. Each dependant of the Indians killed received 500 rupees per body. The Indian National Congress bought the Jallianwalla Bagh as a memorial to the dead.

Details are also to be found in Nigel Collett's *The Butcher of Amritsar* (Hambledon, 2005). Amritsar earns its place in Geoffrey Regan's *Great Military Blunders* (André Deutsch, 1991, many reprints). In the same volume, a piece on *The My Lai Massacre* of 1968 makes the familiar point that the soldiers were as usual 'just following orders'.

The development of the holiday travel industry into escorted cultural tours has taken advantage of some of the rich and diverse opportunities offered by India, and the English traveller may now reserve a place on a tour that embraces Rajasthan, the Taj Mahal and Amritsar's Golden Temple, including a visit to 'the poignant site of the Amritsar massacre'.

Page 91: Nanking ('Nanjing'), 1937

Japan had occupied Manchuria in 1931, and between 1937 - 1945, before China emerged as a major power, Japan and China engaged in continuous war. The Japanese were under military rule. Children were regimented and indoctrinated into strict obedience to serve the Emperor and the Empire. While the military council used Emperor Hirohito as a mouthpiece on account of his semi-divine authority over the people, the military engaged in mass destruction in China and slaughter of the Chinese. The massacre at Nanking was the most notorious episode, in which 150,000 Chinese civilians were killed in the name of the Emperor. See Max Hastings, *All Hell Let Loose: The World at War, 1939-45* (HarperPress, 2011), in which the Nanking episode is seen as a precursor of mass killings in Europe. For a personal account of life under Japanese rule, see *Wild Swans, Three Daughters of China*, by Jung Chang (HarperCollins, 1991). For internal Chinese politics during that period, see *China, New Age and Outlook* (Penguin, 1956), by Ping-chia Kuo. Further detail is available on the internet.

Two films present the Nanking massacre from different viewpoints: the German *City of War* (2010) and the Chinese *City of Life and Death* (2011), each commemorating the horror of 1937. It was entirely consistent that Japan allied herself to Germany during the Second World War, and when, independently, on 7 December 1941, Japan launched a sudden attack on the US fleet in Pearl Harbor, her militarism became destined to play itself out in a ruinous conflict, ending in the catastrophe of 1945.

Page 93: Oradour-sur-Glâne and Distomo, 10 June 1944

Oradour-sur-Glâne was a village commune near Limoges in Haut-Vienne, in Western France, and Distomo was and is near Delphi in Greece. Though geographically widely distant, both names stand for brutal reprisals exacted arbitrarily on village communities under German occupation during the Second World War. There were others. Lord Russell of Liverpool with his *The Scourge of the Swastika, a Short History of Nazi War Crimes* (Transworld, 1954) earned the reputation of an author seeking to shock, but his use of original sources for the massacre at Oradour-sur-Glâne gives support to the view that certainly in this case he had no cause to exaggerate. It is the factual and uncontested content that is inherently shocking.

As part of the campaign against the French Resistance movement, the massacre of 600 innocent people at Oradour-sur-Glâne took place after D-Day while the Allies were already in Normandy. Lord Liverpool quotes first-hand accounts in detail by named survivors of the massacre, accounts which later became part of an official report, and follows with similar incidents, before turning his attention to Italy and the massacre in the Ardeatine Caves in Rome. Field-Marshal Kesselring's orders for reprisals against partisans in 1944, leading to yet more indiscriminate killing, are quoted verbatim. Such incidents in Poland, where the majority of executions took place without trial or sentence, are too numerous even to be listed here. It is regrettable that Lord Russell failed to give names, dates or corroboration for many of the atrocities that he reported having taken place in Poland, and though many of these reports may have been true, and though the truth may have been even worse than reported, he was and still is discredited as an authority.

After the war, Greece made a claim against Germany for compensation for the deaths of thousands of Greeks under Nazi occupation, recorded also at Kalavrita, and in 1960 Germany made a significant payment to the Greek state in settlement. But the survivors and relatives of survivors at Distomo, where

218 were murdered, continued to claim that they were never compensated.

Page 95: Hans Friedrich and Yad Vashem
The interview with Hans Friedrich on which these lines are based was recorded live and incorporated in a TV programme which has been repeated several times on the *Yesterday* TV Channel, including 27 December 2010 and twice in October 2014. It appears in a series on the Second World War with Professor Sir Ian Kershaw as Historical Script Consultant, with other consultants including Professor Christopher Browning, and Samuel West as narrator. It is dated 2005, with the title *Auschwitz: the Nazis and the Final Solution 1/6*. It is a BBC/KCET Hollywood Co-production, written and produced by Laurence Rees, and may be found at bbc.co.uk.history ; for first-hand impressions one may go back even further to the liberation of the camps as documented by news footage, some of which was co-edited by Alfred Hitchcock in 1945 and broadcast on TV in 2015.

Hans Friedrich was a soldier in the 1st SS Infantry Brigade and the victims were from the Jewish community at Ostrog, north-east of Lvov in the Ukraine. His orders came from Himmler. Hans Friedrich believed that Jewish traders, earlier, had cheated him and his family. Towards the end of the interview he says, 'My hatred towards the Jews was too great. I admit my thinking on this point was unjust.' The impression he gives is of having become completely desensitised.

Similar first-hand admissions of mentally detached and cold-blooded killings have been recorded elsewhere. In *Soldaten: On Fighting, Killing and Dying*, by Sonke Neitzel and Harald Weizer (Alfred A.Knopf, 2012), SS Oberscharführer Fritz Swoboda is recorded as having admitted to shooting five or six hundred people day after day. In his documentary film *Shoah* (1985, 566 mins), Claude Lanzmann includes interviews both with survivors of the death camps and with some of the willing perpetrators.

The film was shown as part of Holocaust Memorial Day and broadcast on BBC4 TV on 25 January and 1 February 2015.

The massacres at Oradour-sur-Glâne and Distomo may be judged as reprisals taken against innocent people, and ranked with the massacre at Lidice, a mining village outside Prague, on 9 and 10 June 1942. Lidice was razed to the ground and its name erased from official records. Here as elsewhere, one name is taken to stand for others.

The same applies to Ostrog, above; Ostrog may be viewed as reflecting the relentless force of the German push eastwards, taking every opportunity to annihilate Jewish citizens in the newly occupied territories. Likewise Lvov near the border with Poland was the scene of a massacre on 30 June 1941; Liepaja in Latvia on 8 and 9 July 1941, of which unofficial German film survives; and the massacre at Babi Yar, the name of a ravine on the outskirts of Kiev, has achieved even greater notoriety, where 33,771 Jews were killed by the SS Sonderkommando using machineguns and sub-machineguns in one week in September 1941. For a factual account see Antony Beevor, *The Second World War* (Weidenfeld and Nicolson, 2012). To which should be added Vilnius, capital of Lithuania, on 16 August, 1941; and Lubny, east of Kiev, on 16 October 1941.

The background to these events was presented in a series of programmes under the title *Annihilation*, broadcast on the *Yesterday* TV channel from 17 February 2015. The next in the series on 24 February covered the establishment of camps at Treblinka, Sobibor and Auschwitz, and the means by which they were developed. This programme included a letter from a young German soldier to his mother (though it was forbidden to reveal such information) in which he expressed his initial shock at discovering the scale of the killing carried out by his comrades.

Inevitably, in any discussion of cold-hearted obedience to brutal orders, one recalls the laboratory experiments carried out by Yale University professor Stanley Milgram in 1963. Attempts to undermine his results by querying his methodology have found some flaws, but no fatal flaw; on the contrary, a near-replication of his experiments in 2007 by another psychologist, Jerry Burger, produced similar results. Those who might wish to question Milgram's conclusions are faced with crushing evidence from real life. While noting that Milgram in 1963 had played to a mood of anti-authoritarianism, Dr Michael Mosley in his BBC4 programme *Obedience to Authority,* broadcast on 9 June 2015, gave credence to Milgram's conclusions. Dr Mosley's timid real-life experiments suggested that social norms encourage compliance in the first place. And Milgram's 'shocking' experiments went far beyond daily life with its habits and customs.

Yad Vashem, meaning 'A Place and a Name', is a memorial to the victims of the Holocaust. It was opened in 1957 on Mount Herzl in West Jerusalem. Years of dedicated research have gone into assembling and documenting the photographs now on exhibition.

The enormity of the crimes committed in what is called the Holocaust has overshadowed the civilised world, to the extent that many writers have felt that fact, in this case, is beyond fiction and could not be engaged with directly. Günter Grass found a form that could contain a powerful fiction dealing obliquely with Nazism in *The Tin Drum*, first published in Germany in 1959 (Secker and Warburg, 1962), and made into a film directed by Volker Schlöndorff (1979). Alan Pakula's film *Sophie's Choice* (1982), starring Meryl Streep, from the novel by William Styron, contains painful key scenes from Auschwitz seen in flashback. Two memorable Oscar-winning films, both based on true stories, deserve recognition here: *Schindler's List* (1993), directed by Steven Spielberg, and *The Pianist,* (2002), directed by Roman Polanski, partly reflecting his own experience. The novel *Austerlitz* by W.G. Sebald (Hamish Hamilton, 2001/Penguin 2002) again takes an oblique approach, as the narrator recounts his quest to discover what happened to his family under Nazism. Martin Amis has engaged with Naziism twice, in different ways, with *Time's Arrow* (1991) and *The Zone of Interest* (2014). This is to distinguish selected fiction from the enormous range of factual biography, autobiography, documentary and official war records, and from the enormous range of films in the war genre supplying dramatic action with production values and an eye on box office receipts.

Page 97: *Sharpeville, 21 March 1960*
Page 99: *Marikana, 16 August 2012*
Page 101: *Rwanda, 1994*
Page 103: *Uganda, 2009*

Though the circumstances differ, these four impressions of tragic events, each symptomatic of a disordered African society, may be taken together as a 'Cry for Africa', to which could be added an account of the ongoing depredations of Boko Haram in Nigeria under an ineffective government. The sources of information are all from the media. And though half a century apart, the massacres at Sharpeville and at the Marikana Mine have some features in common. Outside the police station in the South African township of Sharpeville, a crowd of several thousand had gathered to protest against the pass laws. The police opened fire on the protesters, killing 50. The platinum mine at Marikana was owned by the company Lonmin (in which both the trade union Unison and the Church of England were shareholders). In 2012, employees at the mine were on strike, demanding a wage increase. A summary of the Report of the Farlam Commission of Inquiry into the events at the Marikana mine was given on BBC News 24 on 14 November 2014. It was not a planned attack. The Report accused the police of acting like 'a paramilitary firing squad', and of cornering miners who were trying to return home, and of pursuing others. 37 miners on strike were killed. The company Lonmin had earlier established a 500-strong force of private security personnel working closely with the police. The company was under pressure over profit margins and also had to please the shareholders. In Rwanda, the conflict between the Hutus and the Tutsis ended in a repressive dictatorship; refer to

The Observer, 3 January 2016.

A new Report, *Children of the Islamic State,* published for Quillian Research, refers to the child soldiers recruited by rebel Charles Taylor in order to seize power in Liberia in 1997, and just as ominously, to a wider danger: the abduction of children by the Islamic State for indoctrination as boy soldiers. The Report was summarised in *The Observer,* 6 March 2016.

Page 105: Batang Kali, 12 December 1948
Batang Kali is a village, sometimes described as a town, in the district of Sulangor, Malaysia, north-west of Kuala Lumpur. Information about the massacre of 24 unarmed villagers by British troops during the Malayan Emergency, and the subsequent appeals for an Inquiry, with delays and British government refusals lasting over sixty years, is culled from *The Guardian,* BBC News, and from a BBC documentary *In Cold Blood,* broadcast on 9 September 1992. Information collated by *Wikipedia* alone might not be judged conclusive; but together with the above, it has added to the suggestion of a prolonged cover-up, with each new detail as it has emerged adding to the case for a prosecution.

While on 4 September 2012 the High Court judges in London upheld a government decision not to hold a public inquiry into the killing, the Court also ruled that Britain was responsible for the killing at Batang Kali. In its written judgement it said, 'There is evidence that supports a deliberate execution of the 24 civilians at Batang Kali.' The question of a public inquiry went before the Court of Appeal in March 2014 (BBC News, 19 March 2014), and the Court announced that it would make a ruling on whether an inquiry will be held.

The saga had earlier provoked an upsurge of patriotic feeling and regimental loyalty on behalf of the Scots Guards, voiced by *The Scotsman*'s front page headline on 14 December 2003: 'Veterans' Fury at 'Malay Massacre' Claim': 'From Waterloo to the Falklands they fought with undoubted bravery and distinction.

But claims of war crimes during a bloody conflict in south-east Asia have resurfaced and threaten to sully the name of the Scots Guards.'

It is the sense that justice is being flouted that lies behind the patient recording of each stage in the saga since 1948, a sense that places itself in direct conflict with *The Scotsman*'s emotive backing for the troops, as though because of their long history and reputation going back to Waterloo, they deserve to remain above the law.

The Independent reported on 19 April 2015 that the decision of the Supreme Court was imminent, with the headline: 'Batang Kali killings: Britain in the dock over 1948 massacre in Malaysia'. But negative pressure continued from the military: 'The outcome has important ramifications for the UK's duty to investigate historical incidents where British security forces have shot civilians. It could also further establish the extent to which the military is subject to human rights laws. Earlier this month, seven former defence chiefs of staff argued that British forces should be exempt from 'creeping legal expansion on to the battlefield'.'

But the military have forgotten that when it is enemies who are alleged to have committed war crimes, the law is needed and is used to place these enemies on trial.

Colin Shindler's *National Service, from Aldershot to Aden: tales from the conscripts 1946-62* (Sphere, 2012), contains memories and anecdotes ranging from the amusing to the absurd, including those of a National Service conscript in Malaya during the Emergency in 1948. Though armed, he was not involved in combat. Conscription to National Service, a euphemism for military service, ended officially on 31 December 1960. Reporting today at first hand, a former soldier who was in Malaya in 1959 had never heard of Batang Kali.

Page 107: 'Bloody Sunday', 30 January 1972
Two years after the disastrous attempt by British soldiers to control a Civil Rights march in Londonderry, Lord Chief Justice

Widgery headed a tribunal that accepted the army's claim that the soldiers had come under fire from IRA gunmen as they entered the Bogside, and that the action of the army was justified. None of the soldiers who opened fire was ever disciplined, and the officers were later decorated by Her Majesty the Queen.

Public demands for a full, fair and impartial inquiry into the deaths of the 13 unarmed civilians who were shot and into the injuries suffered by another 27 protesters, an Inquiry that, had it taken place, would have given a hearing to a great many witnesses, had come to nothing. There appeared to be concern that the soldiers might be identified and might have to give evidence.

The same concern limited the scope of Lord Saville's Inquiry which began in 1998 and finally reported in 2010. It reversed many of the judgements of the Widgery tribunal but cleared senior military officers of blame. General Ford 'neither knew nor had reason to know at any stage that his decision (to deploy soldiers to arrest rioters) was likely to result in soldiers firing indiscriminately that day'. And so these official Inquiries succeeded in exonerating the military commanders while failing to satisfy the civilians who demanded an independent Inquiry led by someone unconnected with the establishment.

It should be added that no Inquiry had been held into a similar incident in Belfast in 1971 when soldiers of the Parachute Regiment shot dead 11 civilians in Ballymurphy. The latest eruption of the Troubles had involved many more deaths than those that were caused on Bloody Sunday, and the sectarian and political conflicts that divided Northen Ireland were far too deep-rooted to be resolved by armed force, least of all by another intervention by British soldiers, seen by the IRA as an army of occupation.

In this turmoil the introduction on 9 August 1971 of internment (that is, arrest and imprisonment without trial, a draconian expedient with echoes of the Second World War) aroused widespread opposition. It was no substitute for negotiation of the kind that finally led to the Good Friday Agreement, however precarious that compromise has proved to be. And so the perception that a travesty of justice was about to be administered by the British, using armed force, was enough to bring out large numbers of legitimate protesters; how many has never been agreed. The orders that were given to the troops were to arrest rioters; control of the route of the march was confused; poor communication, in an age before the universal use of mobile phones, was partly to blame; but one would have thought that responsibility for the rules of engagement lay with higher authority in the first place, not with the individual soldier, likewise the use of real bullets instead of rubber bullets used for riot control. After that, the mental disconnect between the simple act of pulling a trigger and awareness of its consequences on the fragile human body falls into a familiar pattern.

When the Saville Inquiry finally did report, Prime Minister David Cameron made a public apology on behalf of the UK for the killings and injuries of 30 January 1972, saying that these were 'unjustified and unjustifiable'. One might add that other injustices had also been involved, in the attempt to rule using internment, and in the one-sided first Inquiry, now discredited.

It would not be surprising if the film *Bloody Sunday*, a Granada film made in 2001 by Paul Greengrass with the assistance of the Irish Film Board and supported by Lottery funding, is eventually taken as a substitute for the full, independent and impartial Inquiry that was needed. It is a reconstruction in the style of *cinéma vérité*. The end credits make no secret of the fact that some scenes and some sequences of dialogue have been invented. But the film is even-handed in two most important respects: it shows how the organisers of the march in support of Civil Rights were unable to control the crowds, and how that loss of control was mirrored by a loss of control among the section commanders of the army; and it shows how tension had mounted steadily on both sides, affecting judgement and behaviour. MP Ivan Cooper (played by James Nesbitt) is shown speaking in favour of non-violence. But when the shooting has already been started by the heavily armed soldiers in full battledress, apparently kitted out for guerilla warfare, some even carrying rifles with bayonets as though they were on a battlefield, we see someone appear from round a corner holding a pistol and about to retaliate, presumably representing the IRA. The shabby and depressed setting of the Bogside with sectarian dividing walls and barbed wire, patrolled by troops in armoured cars and using water cannon, is by implication a setting destined to provoke resentment, hostility and violence; there was never going to be any meaningful dialogue or reconciliation in an urban nightmare like this. The film has been shown on ITV on 1 November 2014 and 6 February 2015.

Amid all the signs that justice had once again been circumvented (a thread running through many of the episodes recounted in *Predators: Reflections on a Theme*, Part 3), it was a cause for astonishment when on 10 November 2015 BBC News reported that detectives had arrested a soldier who had taken part in the 'Bloody Sunday' killings 43 years earlier, followed on 17 December by the report that a court had decided not to detain *or question* seven soldiers in N. Ireland but that they could be *interviewed* on the mainland (my italics).

Page 105: Srebenica, 10 July 1995
As this piece is a blend of fiction and circumstantial detail, any introduction must give way to a tribute to the work of the poet Tony Harrison, whose real-life dispatches from Bosnia appeared on the front page of his sponsor *The Guardian*. Imagination defers to first-hand *reportage*. See also Tony Harrison's film-poems, including *In the Shadow of Hiroshima* (1995), made for Channel 4 TV to commemorate the 50th anniversary of the atomic bombing. In his words, 'I've always struggled to find a way of uniting my celebratory nature with a way of seeing horrors clearly'. His *Collected Film Poetry* is published by Faber; his *Collected Poems* are published by Viking. *Three Bosnian Poems*

are in *Selected Poems* (Penguin).

Srebenica is north-east of Sarajevo, which suffered likewise under siege during the Balkan wars. Tuzla is northwest and Mostar is south-west of Srebenica. For a concise account of the wars see Tony Yudt, *Postwar, A History of Europe since 1945* (Pimlico, 2007), pp.674-8.

As the former Yugoslavia disintegrated, the conflict between Bosnian Serbs and Muslim Croatians began in April 1992 accompanied by a violent campaign of 'ethnic cleansing' of non-Serbs. Non-Serbs were held in terrible conditions in camps while at the same time Serbs were held in camps by the Muslim and Croatian authorities. The establishment of a separate Croatia turned the Croats against the Muslims, who were penned into East Mostar and subjected to merciless bombardment. The mainly Muslim inhabitants of Srebenica were held under siege by the Serbian forces and finally expelled or deported. The massacre of 8,000 men and boys at or near Srebenica took place on or near 10 July 1995, and is remembered at each anniversary. The so-called 'death march' to Tuzla, now called the *Mars Mira,* was an exodus of refugees hoping to reach a refugee camp at Tuzla nearly 100 km away where there was a UN air base. It is now commemorated by an annual Peace March in the reverse direction. Of an estimated 15,000 who set out in 1995, only 3,500 reached Tuzla, the remainder having been targeted on the way by heavily armed Serbian soldiers. Those who surrendered were executed.

These and other war crimes were all the more shocking because a UN 'Protection Force' of 14,000 observers had arrived in Bosnia and failed to intervene. A few hundred UN peacekeepers were inserted into selected towns, but with instructions to remain neutral, they ended as passive observers of the shelling of towns and killing of citizens by snipers. Some were held hostage. When the war ended in 1995 it left a legacy of hate and a sense of injustice that remains unresolved. The former Bosnian Serb leader and President of Republika Srpska, Radovan Karadzic, went into hiding but was found and arrested 10 years later and taken to the International Court of Justice at The Hague for trial on charges of war crimes. The trial was spun out over several years. A reporter from *The Observer* interviewed Karadzic in 2011 only to be told that evidence about crimes against humanity at the camps was 'fabricated'. In 2015 the International Court of Justice delivered its verdict on the claim made by each side that the other side was guilty of genocide; both claims were dismissed. Finally, in March 2016, Karadzic was declared guilty of genocide and war crimes and sentenced to 40 years' imprisonmemt.

For a graphic account of the March to Tuzla, quoting from survivors, see the news report posted online by the *Daily Mail* on 6 August 2011. *In the Land of Blood and Honey*, a film made by Angelina Jolie and taking the conflict as its background, was released in 2011. Besides directing this film (her first as director) and having an outstanding career as an actor, Ms Jolie has a role as a goodwill ambassador for the UN High Commission on Refugees. Her film was criticised by a Bosnian Serb authority, who had not seen it, for presenting the Bosnian Serbs as guilty. Critics who have seen the film have taken a different view and applauded it as a sensitive portrayal of a love affair arising in the camps, cutting across the political and religious enmities that fuelled the conflict.

The 20th anniversary of the massacre at Srebenica was commemorated in various ways with varying reactions. On 6 July 2015, BBC 1 broadcast a documentary entitled *A Deadly Warning: Srebenica Revisited,* giving an account of a visit by a mixed group of students, some of whom were relatively ignorant of the tragedy of 1995. The group included the daughter of a UN commander. They visited the Potocari cemetery and memorial centre and saw sombre lists of names on a granite memorial. The students' visit also included a meeting with a Serb official who deflected questions by referring to the killing of Serbs prior to 1995. He had not visited the cemetery, and disagreed with the term 'genocide'. On 12 July 2015, the Serbian Prime Minister, in a gesture of reconciliation, attended the funeral of another 136 victims whose remains had been gathered together, after having apparently been scattered deliberately, and were now about to be buried alongside the mass grave at the memorial centre. He laid flowers and signed a book of condolences. But it was widely reported that the Prime Minister was then chased away by an angry crowd. On 9 August 2015 *The Observer* gave a full page to discoveries of 'hundreds of other mass graves'. The article by Ed Vulliamy was headed: 'Bosnia's survivors gather and grieve as the soil endlessly gives up its dead'.

The aftermath of the war and the survivors' need to memorialise their loss are brought together in *Srebenica in the Aftermath of Genocide,* by Lara J.Nettelfield and Sarah E.Wagner (Cambridge, 2014). The genocide at Srebenica during 1995, under the direction of General Ratko Mladic, is summarised on pp.8-14, with a brief reference to the march to Tuzla. While the problems of returnees and of postwar reconciliation create a paradigm of unresolved conflict, the national and international issues raised by the war in Bosnia and the failed intervention by the UN have become a *cause célèbre* in international law. There is an increasing flow of publications dealing with international law and human rights that need to supervene over local politics.

From a different point of view, the 'War Child' movement and charity, with its background in the war between Muslims and Serbs, was covered in an article in *The Observer* for 4 July 2010, referring to both East Mostar and Srebenica.

Page 113: Desiderata

The title usually refers to desirable virtuous qualities. Here it refers to less desirable requirements or pre-conditions recurring throughout history; when these coincide, there will be the familiar consequences. Karen Armstrong, in *Fields of Blood: Religion and the History of Violence* (Bodley Head, 2014) argues that violence may be embedded in the human psyche. In a commentary reaching deep into the past and ranging worldwide, she shows how violence has alway been part of human society and how an ideology, especially in the hands of fanatical adherents, can be the driver. Karen Armstrong attributes violence to the 'reptilian' instinct in the human species, so that religion (in its broadest sense) may escape the common accusation of responsibility for violence. She is not alone in discovering primal animal instincts hidden in the human psyche.

But when religious movements or groups adopt violence to achieve power, the release of primal animal instincts is in practice inseparable from their beliefs and behaviour; their behaviour is an expression of their beliefs; the one intensifies the other; 'religion', as the term is used and understood, cannot escape responsibility for the consequences. Perhaps the argument was a case of special pleading. Religion does not appear to serve as a check on violence. It has often been an intensifier. See the earlier comment on 'holy war' under *Jerusalem: The First Crusade,* and refer to the history of the First World War for the attempts by some clergy, a minority, to represent that conflict as a 'holy war'.

Epilogue

Page 117:
Remembrance Sunday *(based on BBC broadcast)*
followed by
The Field of Poppies at the Tower of London,
The Unknown Civilian
and
The Empty Plinth.

A running commentary on the Remembrance Sunday Ceremony at the Cenotaph in 2015 was delivered for the BBC by David Dimbleby. His blend of informality and respect hit all the right notes, natural simplicity being the key. For this reason, the opening sentence from his commentary has been gratefully borrowed and used to introduce the word-picture given here.

The need to express both public and private grief at the deaths of servicemen in war is symbolised by the Cenotaph in Whitehall, the war memorial designed by Sir Edward Lutyens – a design much copied or adapted in many other countries. The Cenotaph was unveiled by King George V on November 14, 1920, as was the tomb of the Unknown Warrior in Westminster Abbey. Cenotaph means 'empty tomb', that of someone who is buried elsewhere. For this event and for a wide-ranging survey of the practice of remembrance in its time, see the final chapter entitled *Remembrance* in Alan Wilkinson's *The Church of England and the First World War* (Lutterworth, 1978/2015). Acts of remembrance may, because of their increasing formality when performed regularly, appear institutional, but in fact have evolved independently; for example, the laying of wreaths was originally a spontaneous act by members of the public. It is worth emphasising that despite the prominence of the Anglican Bishop of London in leading a short religious service alongside the Cenotaph, as a memorial the Cenotaph has no religious affiliation; it is not an altar; there is no Anglican rite of remembrance; it was never intended as a religious monument. In any case, the design of the Cenotaph has pre-Christian connotations, neo-Assyrian and Babylonian, and the iconography of wreaths recalls classical Greece and Rome. Lutyens was active in the War Graves Commission, which respected all faiths and all nations, in the interests of common humanity. It should be added that the commemoration on Remembrance Sunday is only one of several annual events based on the Cenotaph, including a more specific commemoration for the Royal Tank Regiment.

Dr Wilkinson's final chapter suggests that healing may be brought about through the expression of grief. Earlier chapters give an account of how the clergy struggled to cope with the extraordinary stresses of the First World War, from the supportive approach to military recruitment in an atmosphere of jingoism and chauvinism, through to the realisation that the 'lovely' war had become an industrial killing machine. The patriotic motivation ended in a sense of futility, memorably expressed in some of the poems of Wilfred Owen. Dr Wilkinson notes from Wilfred Owen's letters that the poet felt that the sufferings of war had brought him nearer to the suffering Christ. Some artists such as James Clark in his *The Great Sacrifice* (1914) made a direct connection between Christ and a soldier's death on the battlefield, a kind of visual sermon that was popularly received. Yet it contradicts Christian teaching. It is Christ's sacrifice, unarmed, not the individual's self-sacrifice, or the armed soldier's death on the battlefield, that is redemptive. There were painful contradictions in the attitude of the Anglican Church to the First World War, and indeed to war itself. In contrast, the Roman Catholic Church knew what it was doing and in August 1917 Pope Benedict XV promulgated a far-sighted peace plan, while Anglican clergy gave sermons with conflicting messages.

Acts of remembrance are traditionally placed in a liturgical framework with a religious service. One such religious service, held on 3 August 2014 to commemorate the First World War, with the participation of civic, military and religious dignitaries and attended by the present writer, included processions, the laying of military standards at a cathedral altar, the Apostle's

Creed (with its theological content quite remote from the mixed and largely secular congregation), The Beatitudes (at odds with the military paraphernalia), The Lord's Prayer (following the Book of Common Prayer in defying the Biblical injunction that The Lord's Prayer is for private use only), a patriotic hymn, the 23rd Psalm, collects and prayers for peace, and the National Anthem. Everything had been thrown into the Order of Service.

Meanwhile, as reported by Ben Quinn and Richard Norton-Taylor in *The Guardian* on 4 August 2014, peace campaigners had been protesting at official commemorations of the First World War, emphasising that 'the route to war was not scripted: there are always choices'. The incongruities in fusing religious and military messages in official commemorations are accentuated when a member of the clergy wears military medals on his surplice. As John Ferguson pointed out in *The Politics of Love: The New Testament and Non-Violent Revolution* (James Clarke, Cambridge, n.d.),

> 'There is no more ironical moment than the moment in Armistice Sunday when the massed soldiers on church parade, the government and opposition of the day, the civic dignitaries, join in singing:
> Sufficient is thine arm alone,
> And our defence is sure.'

For Armistice Sunday read Remembrance Sunday, though the latter came first on this occasion. These words, from 'O God our help in ages past', are by the nonconformist preacher and writer Isaac Watts and the hymn tune known as *St Anne* is probably by William Croft, organist to the Chapel Royal and later Westminster Abbey, and composer to Queen Anne. At the 2015 Remembrance Sunday commemoration held at the Cenotaph, this deservedly popular hymn seemed to retain an ability to register with a secular audience. The music is from the list of 16 pieces traditionally performed at this ceremony since 1930. Some of the other pieces with links or suggested links to the might and glory of the British Empire, such as Thomas Arne's *Rule, Britannia* (1740), are beginning to sound incongruous. Does it matter? Of course it does, in the presence of 46 members of the Commonwealth and Overseas Territories. Are all traditions good, simply because they are traditions?

An incongruity occurs in the use of the finest piece of all, *Nimrod*, from Elgar's *Enigma Variations* (1899). Michael Kennedy's *The Oxford Dictionary of Music* reminds us that it is often used as a commemorative separate item, and one might add, that it is used in an arrangement for a purpose, and to create a mood, though it prefers the original orchestration. In the context of a Remembrance Day parade the mood is solemn, heroic, grandiose, and emotively patriotic, alongside the monument whose only inscription is 'The Glorious Dead'. A. J. Jaeger (Nimrod) was Elgar's close friend and not a dead soldier. A massed military band and the attendance of guards with fixed bayonets turns the late Victorian Elgar into a militarist, which he was not. He was far removed from the First World War. Later, as Percy Young wrote in his *Elgar, O.M.* (Collins, 1955), 'The special characteristic of Elgar's wartime music was not patriotism so much as pity.'

A further incongruity, again related to the emotive power of music, arises in the powerful link between a tune and a poem, of which we do not hear the words. The well- known tune, known as *The Supreme Sacrifice*, was written by Rev. C. Harris for a poem by the diplomat Sir John Stanhope Arkwright, published in 1922. It is a tune that has become inseparable from the text, as follows:

1 O valiant hearts, who to your glory came,
2 Through dust of conflict and through battle flame
5 Proudly you gathered, rank on rank to war,
6 As who had heard God's message from afar
21 These were His servants, in His steps they trod,
22 Following through death the martyred Son of God;
23 Victor, He rose; victorious too shall rise
24 They who have drunk His cup of sacrifice.

The tune that instantly evokes these religiose words was played to accompany the entry of the small boys of the Choir of the Chapel Royal. It is difficult to separate remembrance from patriotism and militarism in public ceremonies. To avoid a discussion of either, that would be unwelcome here, it is best to leave the last words to Nurse Edith Cavell: 'I realise that patriotism is not enough. I must have no hatred or bitterness towards anyone.' (12 December, 1915). The *Prayer for generosity* of St Ignatius Loyola (1491-1556) was read out in full by the Bishop of London as follows:

> To give and not to count the cost,
> To fight and not to heed the wounds,
> To toil and not to seek for rest,
> To labour and not to ask for any reward
> Save knowing that we do Thy will.'

And it is much used on other occasions. Another note on the music: Sir Henry Walford Davies, who composed Solemn Melody (1908) for organ and cello, also composed the music for a number of hymns and, while he was the RAF music director, music for an RAF March-Past (1917). Davies had a long career as Master of the King's Music and in work with the BBC.

For the march-past on Remembrance Sunday, the musical arrangements are linked to provide a seamless forward-moving accompaniment, with some wartime allusions.

That the commemoration of the dead in the First World War or any war need not be based on a religious service, or within a church of any one denomination, or need use a liturgy that may be divisive, was demonstrated on 3 August 2015 by a ceremony held at the St Symphorien Cemetery in Mons, close to the site of the first engagement of the British Expeditionary Force on 23 August 1914. Jon Henley, in the edition of *The Guardian* quoted above, described it as a 'simple and intimate ceremony' and 'a slickly choreographed but often beautiful and moving service'. It was narrated by Dan Snow, was shown on BBC2, and included the laying of flowers, readings, poetry and music, in which children took an active part. The point was that the St Symphorien cemetery contains the headstones of 284 German as well as 229 British and Commonwealth soldiers. As if to drive home the message of reconciliation across national boundaries, the ceremony was attended by Germany's President Joachim Gauck, King Philippe of Belgium, The Duke and Duchess of Cambridge, Prince Harry, and Prime Minister David Cameron.

Page 127: The Field of Poppies at the Tower of London
This piece is not an impression at first hand. The present writer would like to read any impressions in verse written at first hand by visitors at the time.

The title refers to the display created by the artist Tom Piper to mark the centenary of the First World War in 2014. The artist's own title was *Bloodswept Sands and Seas of Red.* It consisted of 88,246 ceramic poppies laid as a tribute to that number of British and Commonwealth soldiers who died between 1914-18. It was freely open to view by members of the public and was remarkable in that, while it was an artist who devised the installation, it was the visitors who, by attending in unexpected numbers to pay their respects, turned it into a temporary national memorial. At the end of each day a reading was given, as in a roll-call, of the names of 180 of those commemorated in the display. After the huge display was dismantled, some parts were preserved for exhibition in museums in London and Manchester (not immediately) and some of the poppies were sold. More than £1 million was raised for each of six charities. The installation had communicated something that 'top-down' commemorations with a pre-conceived liturgical framework would find it difficult to do.

It was all the more moving because the display was silent, without massed brass bands, field guns, speeches or hymns. It had touched the popular imagination in a way that, spontaneously and unofficially, turned it into a truly shared memorial.

But if war memorials are concerned primarily with

remembering soldiers who served in the armed forces, they are meeting only half the need for remembrance. Modern war is just as deadly in killing civilians as it is in killing soldiers, airmen and sailors, if not more so. Civilians are killed in their millions.

Page 129: The Unknown Civilian
This piece was prompted by the opening of the Bomber Command Memorial in June 2012 on the edge of Green Park in central London. The temple-like structure houses a statuary group commemorating the heavy loss of life among the bomber crew who carried out bombing missions over Germany during the Second World War. 55,573 airmen were lost on these missions, almost as many as the victims of German bombing over England. An equally controversial memorial had been opened at Lincoln Cathedral in August 2006.

The bombing of German cities for non-military purposes was controversial even during wartime. On 9 February 1944 Bishop Bell spoke in the House of Lords against the policy of bombing German cities, reminding his listeners that we were supposed to stand for civilised values. Prime Minister Winston Churchill, who had originally approved this strategy, turned against it. Though a statue was erected post-war in the Strand to Air Marshal 'Bomber' Harris, notwithstanding the vainglorious promise he had made to end the war in six weeks, a promise that was proved both costly and wrong, there was prolonged resistance to honouring those who dropped the bombs.

Bombing civilians in cities, by both sides, may be considered a war crime. The moral issues lying behind the Bomber Command Memorial in Green Park, as well as the nature of its design, were raised by the architectural reviewer Rowan Moore in *The Observer* on 24 June 2012, under the headline 'A monument to obliviousness: There's a jarring lack of sensitivity in this clumsy tribute,' commenting: 'It is an inadvertent echo of the fixed thinking that directed the flattening of German cities.'

For further light on the policy and practice of dropping bombs on civilians, see B.H. Liddell Hart, *History of the Second*

World War (Cassell, 1970), Ch.33: *The Crescendo of Bombing – The Strategic Air Offensive Against Germany;* and Max Hastings, *Bomber Command* (Pan Military Classics, 1979). The grim day-to-day details of aircrew losses and their circumstances are collated in 7 volumes by W.R. Chorley, *RAF Bomber Command: Losses of the Second World War* (Midland, various dates). See also Sven Lindquist, *A History of Bombing* (Granta Books, 2000). A programme *Turning the Tide,* from the series *World War II In Colour,* on Britain and America's strategy to destroy Germany's infrastructure through repeated bombing raids on its cities, was broadcast on Channel 5 TV on 24 and 25 October 2014. The 70th anniversary of the destruction of Dresden and its civilian population in a fire-storm caused by bombing with incendiaries was commemorated in Germany on 13 February 2015. There are numerous studies in fact and faction of this war crime, notably Kurt Vonnegut's *Slaughterhouse Five* (1963). For an assessment of its purpose and usefulness, see Frederick Taylor, *Dresden, 13 February 1945* (Bloomsbury, 2004), correcting some of the suspect figures in David Irving's *The Destruction of Dresden* (1963). Irving's book did have a special value but his status as a historian was undermined by his later stance as a Holocaust-denier. A German commission reporting in 2010 reduced the figures for those killed at Dresden to 25,000, fewer than those killed in Hamburg in 1943. The figures matter, without answering the criticism that the policy of area bombing for non-military purposes undermined the values of civilisation, and that its execution was a crime that has never been justified. See A.C. Grayling's *Among the Dead Cities: The History and Moral Legacy of the WWII Bombing of Civilians in Germany and Japan* (Bloomsbury, 2006).

The piece entitled *The Unknown Civilian* is not to be confused with W.H. Auden's poem *The Unknown Citizen,* which has an entirely different theme and is concerned to show the degree of conformity exercised by society and imposed by the state on the individual.

Page 131: The Empty Plinth

The theme of this piece echoes the roll-calls read out each evening at the *Bloodswept Sands and Seas of Red* installation at the Tower of London during November 2014 (see above). Both this piece and *The Unknown Civilian* are intended to shift attention towards the civilian victims of war who died or suffered in their millions and are much more likely to be forgotten. 'Every autocrat' - an expansion of Lord Acton's celebrated aphorism: 'Power tends to corrupt, and absolute power corrupts absolutely.'

With acknowledgements to Bob Dylan for the closing line and also for his ironic *With God on Our Side,* which links to other pieces in *Predators: Reflections on a Theme.* In 2016 Dylan was awarded the Nobel Prize in Literature.

Footnote

There is extensive coverage of World War II in the long- running series entitled *The World at War,* produced by Jeremy Isaacs and narrated with sober respect and restraint by Sir Laurence Olivier. The consultant was Noble Frankland, director of the Imperial War Museum. Episodes are frequently broadcast on TV. The episode most closely related to the *Epilogue* above is entitled *Remembrance,* is dated 1967, and was broadcast again on the *Yesterday* Channel on Christmas Day, 2015.

The voice-over commentary pays special attention to the indiscriminate killing of innocent civilians during wartime, and points out that these killings followed on decisions 'taken at the highest level.' It was only one of many, but singled out as worthy of special remembrance is the massacre at Oradour-sur-Glâne *(see above,* p.93 and p.182). The narrator constantly calls on the listener and viewer to 'Remember... remember... remember...'

Appendix

Page 79, Page 173

The wording of the original blue plaque (beneath the crest of Manchester City Council) was as follows:

THE SITE OF ST PETER'S FIELDS
WHERE ON 16th AUGUST 1819 HENRY HUNT,
RADICAL ORATOR, ADDRESSED AN
ASSEMBLY OF ABOUT 60,000 PEOPLE. THEIR
SUBSEQUENT DISPERSAL BY THE MILITARY
IS REMEMBERED AS 'PETERLOO'

After a campaign of objections, it was replaced in 2007 by a red plaque, with wording (beneath an icon of a horseman riding down a woman) as follows:

ST PETER'S FIELDS THE PETERLOO MASSACRE
ON 16TH AUGUST 1819 A PEACEFUL RALLY OF 60,000
PRO-DEMOCRACY REFORMERS, MOSTLY IMPOVERISHED
WORKERS AND THEIR FAMILIES, WAS CHARGED
BY ARMED CAVALRY RESULTING IN 11 DEATHS AND
OVER 500 SEVERE INJURIES

Cruikshank's satirical cartoon shows a magistrate holding a tipped pair of scales (justice!) and exclaiming, 'Cut them down, don't be afraid, they are not armed. Courage my boys and you shall have a vote of thanks and he that Kills shall be made a Knight errant and your exploits shall live for ever as a song in verse Chivey Chase (Chevy Chase was the epic medieval war-ballad set on the border between Northumberland and Scotland). Orator Hunt exclaims 'Murder, murder, Malpractice', while the Yeomen cry 'None but the brave deserve the Fair' and 'Cut him down, cut him down', and a small boy appeals, 'O pray Sir, don't kill Mammy, she only came to see Mr Hunt'.